H. H. Munro (Saki)

By CHARLES H. GILLEN

Twayne Publishers, Inc. :: New York

Library of Congress Catalog Card Number: 78-99544

ISBN 0-8057-1408-1

MANUFACTURED IN THE UNITED STATES OF AMERICA

Preface

H. H. Munro must be accounted one of the most grievous losses that English literature suffered in World War I, if only because through his work he brought a badly needed gaiety and an excruciating funniness into a dreary and literal-minded world. Critics have usually fastened upon Munro's idiosyncratic ability to comment perceptively and ironically on the foibles of the topmost people in Great Britain during the pre-1914 age of conspicuous consumption. Of course this characteristic is quite true: there was no shrewder observer of the idle, privileged, frivolous caste which then adorned British society. But Munro was several other things too, and this study attempts to show the determination with which he ventured into other fields of writing and the innate ability which enabled him to win a measure of success as a versatile writer.

Munro turned his hand to just about every kind of literary endeavor. He began his writing career as a historian, then produced political journalism, next created the first of the short stories which keep his name alive today, followed these with service as a foreign correspondent to a great London newspaper, next wrote two novels and a play, and finally—again as a political journalist—reported on the sessions of the House of Commons just before the outbreak of World War I. Munro was truly the all-around man of letters.

His birth into the upper middle class and the special way in which it formed his character are discussed. After an examination of his first book, *The Rise of the Russian Empire,* and an account of a professional historian's dismissal of it, this study turns to Munro's advent in Fleet Street with the *Westminster Alice* and *Not So Stories* which foreshadowed his preoccupation with British politics. His later short stories are discussed with emphasis on how they were shaped by Munro's own rather rarefied background. His five years as a foreign correspondent are investigated in some detail, as is his newspaper material, an aspect rarely, if ever, discussed. His first novel, *The Unbearable Bassington,* is considered from the position that it was Munro's demonstration of his ability to compose fiction of greater length than the short story; and his second novel, *When William Came,* is treated as his personal contribution to the campaign for universal military service in prewar Britain. His play, *The Watched Pot,* is shown to indicate his promise as a playwright; and finally, his versatility and dependability as a journeyman journalist are shown in a sampling of his odd jobs for various periodicals.

The comments, observations, and analyses in this study have been reinforced by many excerpts from Munro's writings; nothing could more clearly demonstrate how clever and able a writer Munro was than their juxtaposition with the text of this book, which hopefully attempts to catch some glints from a literary jewel.

CHARLES H. GILLEN

Acknowledgments

I should like to thank the Viking Press, Inc., for permission to quote from Munro's books and from their Introductions.

I should also like to thank Mr. J. W. Lambert for permission to quote from his Introduction to the *Bodley Head Saki*.

Acknowledgment is due to A. D. Peters & Co. for permission to quote from Evelyn Waugh's Introduction to *The Unbearable Bassington*.

Contents

Chronology

1870 Hector Hugh Munro born on December 18 in Akyab, Burma. His mother died soon afterward.

1873 Brought by his father, a major in the British Army, to Pilton, Devonshire, England, to be reared by the father's two sisters and mother. Hector's elder sister and brother, Ethel and Charles, were also turned over to these guardians for upbringing. Although Hector was a sickly child, he was given at Pilton a strict, rather impersonal upbringing which is generally believed to be the most formative influence upon his character.

1878 Hector's father came home on leave from India to visit his children.

1882 The father again returned to England on leave.

1883 Hector studied at Broadgate with the governess who had been chosen for his sister.

1884 Hector went away to Pencarwick School in Exmouth "and was very happy there."

1885 In September Hector attended Bedford School, Bedfordshire, an old public school. Extremely formative and influential experience, à la "the old school tie."

1886 Left Bedford School in December.

1887 Hector's father retired from the army; took Ethel and Hector on trip to Etretat in France.

1889 Munro père took Ethel and Hector for a second trip to the Continent. They visited Dresden, Berlin, Munich, Nuremberg, Prague, and Innsbruck, and then settled for the winter in Switzerland at Davos.

1890 The Munros left Davos in April and returned to England. They took a house in Heanton, Devonshire. Brother Charlie went to Burma to join the police.

1891– 1892 Hector and Ethel studied for two years at Heanton under the father's direction. Hector roamed freely about the Devon countryside. At the end of 1892 the Munros returned to Davos in Switzerland.

1893 The Munros returned to England in the spring. In May, Hector went out to Burma to join the Military Police, a post obtained for him by his father. Hector conscientiously took up his duties as a traveling mounted policeman.

1894 During the summer, the final bout of seven attacks of malaria so weakened Hector that he had to resign from the police and return to England. The Munros now lived at Westward Ho! in Devonshire, where Hector convalesced.

1895 Slow convalescence in Devonshire. Hector deepened his knowledge of the Devon people and countryside.

1896 Hector left Devonshire for London "to earn his living by writing."

1897– 1898 A period of attempting to break into the field of letters. Occasional trips back to bosom of family at Westward Ho!

1899 Composing *The Rise of the Russian Empire.*

1900 *The Rise of the Russian Empire* published. Munro and F. Carruthers Gould collaborated on the *Westminster Alice,* published in the *Westminster Gazette.*

1902 Collaborated with Gould on the *Not So Stories* for the *Westminster Gazette.* The *Westminster Alice* published in book form. Became foreign correspondent for the London *Morning Post* in Bulgaria, Macedonia, and other parts of the Balkans.

1903 *Reginald* stories appeared in *Westminster Gazette.*

1904 Foreign correspondent in Serbia and Poland. *Reginald* published in book form. Correspondent in St. Petersburg.

1905 Witnessed "Bloody Sunday" in St. Petersburg; reported on Russian revolution of 1905.

1906 Reported on opening of first Russian Duma. Went to Paris as correspondent of *Morning Post.*

1907 Summoned to England because of father's death. Returned to France as correspondent.

1908 Gave up correspondent's job and returned to England. Took lodgings in London; bought a house in Caterham on the Surrey Hills.

1909 Final phase of career, when he earned living solely as freelance writer. Steadily contributed short stories to the *Morning Post*, the *Westminster Gazette*, and the *Bystander*, as well as occasional journalistic work, until 1914.

1910 *Reginald in Russia.*

1911 *Chronicles of Clovis.*

1912 *The Unbearable Bassington.*

1913 *When William Came.*

1914 Coming to close of collaboration with Cyril Maude on the play *The Watched Pot.* Reported on Parliament for the *Outlook. Beasts and Super-Beasts* published in June. Volunteered on the outbreak of war in August, joining the 2nd King Edward's Horse. Found cavalry life too strenuous; transferred to the infantry to the 22nd Battalion Royal Fusiliers.

1915 Underwent infantry training at Horsham, Clipstone, and Tidworth in England. In November, went into combat in France.

1916 Participated in several military actions, including first Vimy Ridge. In June, went to London on leave. Returned to France to participate in the Delville Wood battle, a part of the Somme offensive. In October, sent to base hospital for treatment of recurrence of malaria. Returned to battalion in time to take part in Beaumont Hamel offensive. Killed in action on November 14.

CHAPTER 1

The Mold

HECTOR HUGH MUNRO was born in Akyab, Burma, on December 18, 1870. His father, C. A. Munro, was a British Army officer, and his mother was a daughter of Rear Admiral Samuel Mercer of the British Navy. Hector's mother died not long after he was born, and the father then brought him and his sister Ethel and his brother Charles, who were older than he, from Burma to England. The father delegated the responsibility of rearing these motherless children to his two maiden sisters, who were assisted by the children's grandmother. The women took the three children as their wards into their home in Devonshire, and Hector's father returned to duty in the East as inspector-general of the Burmese Police, detached from the Bengal Staff Corps.[1]

The Munro children were brought up at Broadgate Villa in the little Georgian community of Pilton, on the outskirts of Barnstaple. Broadgate, in the beautiful coastal country of North Devon, was a rather imposing eighteenth-century house with a southern exposure and three bow windows.[2] The house overlooked the slopes of a large lawn which sported a flower garden among the scattered elms, and in back were a walled-in garden and a greenhouse. Ethel wrote of *two* nurseries there; of servants, governesses, a contract gardener, a family doctor; and of pets which included tortoises, rabbits, doves, guinea pigs, cats, and poultry. Altogether, it was the sort of well-to-do home in which very few people of that time—or of today, for that matter—had the great good fortune to spend their childhood.

But sister Ethel drew the picture of an unhappy household at Broadgate vitiated by the incapabilities of the aunts who, she wrote, performed ineptly as guardians while pettishly quarreling with each other as grandmother Munro looked supinely on. The aunts were psychologically unequipped to raise children, Ethel claimed; and their unfailing strictness harmfully worked a repression upon her and her two brothers that warped their formative years.[3] This theme of stultification through unnecessary harshness, recurring throughout Ethel's biographical sketch, is believed by most critics to be the basic cause of the inhumanity and impassive cruelty so evident in Munro's writing.[4] Munro himself added to the legend of an unloved and somehow deprived childhood in two of his best-known short stories, "The Lumber Room" and "Sredni Vashtar."

In actuality, Munro was fortunate in his heritage. Although he lost his mother while he was still an infant, he was the inheritor of something that may be worth more in the world than a mother's tender presence: he was born into the upper levels of his society, into that British caste of breeding, preference, and privilege known as "the Establishment." Munro was born one of the favored few for whom the whole Imperial system turned its massive clockwork, and his military heritage insured his acceptance into the little band of the Empire's rulers.

It was not necessary to be wealthy—Munro never was—to fit comfortably into the mold of a public school and to follow the smoothed path into one of the right professions. Wealth was not too important in the Establishment: breeding, descent, line of birth were everything. In today's more nearly perfect democracy, it is difficult to appreciate the scope of prestige and preferential treatment enjoyed by the true "gentleman." The belittling of the Establishment would have been incomprehensible in the time of Munro's youth, when the world was stable and everyone had his fixed place in it. What better luck could one then have had than to be born at the top level?

The Broadgate regime was at times not too bad, Ethel admitted handsomely. The children were "delicate," and the evidence indicates a heritage of tuberculosis from the mother. Hector was the most fragile of the lot. "The aunts nursed him carefully," Ethel wrote. "We had only to be ill and everything was changed at Broadgate, scolding was a thing of the past." [5] Yet Hector was not precisely a sickly child, to judge by the biography's descriptions of his forays into the forbidden kitchen garden, "leaping at the nearest boy" pugnaciously on the rather rare occasions when he mingled with other children, and riding pigs and climbing haystacks during his father's home leaves from the East.

Still, it was an odd sort of existence for the three semi-orphans. Much of the time was spent unhealthily indoors, although Ethel wrote that "we should have had more country walks than we ever got, there were lovely fields and woods quite handy." [6] The isolation turned Hector in upon himself for mental and spiritual resources, and he early developed the habit of serious reading. Broadgate's was certainly not the usual sort of household atmosphere for growing children, but the memories of it in afterlife were not all unhappy. "He once said to me," wrote Ethel, "that in spite of our strict upbringing and having no other children to play with, he was glad of it, as otherwise we should never have been original." [7]

I *Imperial Nursery*

Elder brother Charles, who enjoyed somewhat better health, was the first to escape the sequestered atmosphere of Broadgate by going to Pencarwick, a boarding school in Exmouth. Hector, kept at home a while longer, studied with his sister's governess; but, when he was fourteen, he followed in Charles's steps to Pencarwick. Ethel wrote that Hector "was very happy there" [8] although his stay was brief. When Charles moved on to Charterhouse, a public school of fairly high standing, Hector, as befitted a younger son, had to settle for a school less exalted in Establishment eyes. In September, 1885, in his fifteenth year, Hector assumed the upper-middle-class birthright of a public school education by entering Bedford School in Bedfordshire. He seems to have accepted uncomplainingly the rather spartan living conditions and the strict discipline that these schools impose upon the sons of the upper classes.

Bedford is a fairly old public school as these institutions go in Great Britain, having been founded in 1552. Attendance there confirmed in Hector his sense of social superiority, of belonging to an elite group; and the school turned Hector out as an obvious member of the gentry with the cool savoir faire that came so effortlessly to the best people. As an influence on his fiction, the Bedford experience was much weightier than his atypical childhood years at Broadgate because he accepted and absorbed the attitudes, postures, and social outlook fostered by the British public school tradition. And beneath the flippancy, the skepticism, the jaundiced snobbery of much of Munro's writing lies the Bedford bedrock of personal honor, of correct behavior, of devotion to duty.

This school, sometimes called a "nursery of the Empire," turned out future officers of the Indian Army and police force with consistency; and its "old boys" used to return from duty in the East to Bedford as sunburned officers to view interschool boat races along the Ousel River.[9] The school, apparently an invaluable instrument in the great task of ruling "the lesser breeds without the law," forced its pupils to participate in entertainments and public speaking.[10] Here, undoubtedly, is the reason why Munro, normally a rather reserved individual, was an unabashed actor in amateur theatricals in afterlife, and why he was able to give orders creditably and to speak with authority and "presence" in his later police force and military phases.

Presumably because of his uncertain health, Munro left Bedford School in December, 1886. The public school experience is not evident in most of Munro's writings, although the second chapter of *The Unbearable Bassington* emphasizes the public school students' methods of disciplining themselves. But there is unobtrusively present in almost everything Munro wrote the acceptance of the precept that one must always keep a stiff upper lip no matter what, the precept which is the end-all of the British public school system.

II *Wanderjahre*

When Munro's father retired from the army as a colonel in 1888, he returned to England to assume at last the dubious pleasure of looking after his children. The old gentleman is described by J. W. Lambert: "He was remarkably handsome, and his manner was courtly; he could and did kiss a woman's hand with no little distinction. After middle age his complexion was fresh, his hair and moustaches white, his manner gentle, quiet and smiling. He smoked cheroots all day." [11] This interesting man, the belatedly involved parent, seemed to be at a loss as to the correct routine of rearing adolescents. First, he took them for a stay in Etretat in Normandy, and then returned with them to England.

He soon went back to the Continent with the children, and Ethel wrote that "Our second trip abroad was a more educational one." [12] They first visited Dresden, "a lengthy stay," after which

Charles, more robust than the other two children, returned to school in England. The father then conducted Ethel and Hector on a tour of central Europe, beginning with Berlin and going on to Nuremberg, Munich, and Prague.

This extensive traveling, besides giving Hector an excellent grounding in conversational French and German, allowed him to absorb the feel and atmosphere of *mitteleuropa* which in later years so often colored his fiction with an authenticity which only participation can give. This tour, too, helped to make Munro the true cosmopolitan he always remained under his occasional Tory insularity. And his admiration for the moneyed, elegant, variegated life in the company of the educated rich and, conversely, his contempt for orderly, cramped, "nine-to-five" living presumably took root during this period.

The Munros ended their tour with a long visit to Switzerland at Davos, which was then favored by many of the British upper-class types who suffered from what was euphemistically called "consumption." The cold, dry air of Davos was thought to have special therapeutic qualities for this ailment, and the fact that the two Munro children were brought there is presumptive evidence of a legacy of tuberculosis. Their life at Davos left a happy memory: Ethel wrote of the tennis, riding, winter sports, and fancy dress balls there with nostalgia. They left Davos in April, 1890, and stayed at "Schloss Salenstein, on the Swiss side of Lake Constance, the home of some very charming people whom we met at Davos," [13] which should give an idea of the rarefied circles in which they moved while abroad.

Brother Charles went out to join the Burmese police, his eyesight being unacceptable to the army; and the remainder of the little family returned to England later on in 1890. They settled in North Devon again, this time in Heanton, "four miles from Barnstaple, also four miles from the aunts." [14] Heanton Court was a big house, "absurdly large for us," Ethel said.[15] It was very old and redolent of English history; a famous writer, R. D. Blackmore, had written of it at length in his *Maid of Sker;* and it was thought to have a number of evil spirits and other bogles lurking about, so that in Hector's eyes it must have been an eminently suitable abode.

III *White Man's Burden*

"For two years we lived at Heanton" wrote Ethel, "studying under my father's direction." [16] The conventional subjects that were included in Munro *pére's* curriculum, the educational bricks and mortar, were not exclusive of the odd interests that Hector was really absorbed in—the offbeat things like heraldry, genealogy, natural history, and ornithology. Because he was allowed to follow congenial bypaths, this formative period is responsible for the odd erudition, the zoological figures of speech, and the literary references from unlikely sources that are sprinkled throughout *The Rise of the Russian Empire,* Munro's first book.

Heanton was Munro's equivalent of a university education, but how much more originally and conscientiously was he instructed there than he would have been at Oxford or Cambridge; and the permissiveness to take to his own byways was far more valuable to him than would have been the unimaginative tour of duty at a university. And the "educated scorn" that H. W. Nevinson said Munro was "endowed with" [17] derived largely from his unique education at Heanton.

The little family of three went to London in the late spring of 1892 to partake in the ritualized pleasures of that months-long house party of the Establishment, the London Season. The sophistication of the drawing room, the dinner table, and the ballroom was the culmination of Hector's education; the glossy and urbane world of fashion that paraded before him was to be his chosen and peculiarly personal corner of English letters.

The Munros returned to Davos for the winter of 1892–93, enjoying the resort even more than on their first visit there. In the spring of 1893, when they returned again to Devonshire, they did not go back to Heanton; they went instead to stay with Aunt Tom, the less offensive of the two former guardians.

The problem of what to do with Hector, the younger and thus less favored son, was becoming embarrassingly acute. His father had put in many years of police service in Burma while on loan from the Bengal Staff Corps in India, and before his retirement he had attained the high rank of inspector-general of police. Although it would be fairly easy for the old gentleman to obtain a post in the Burmese military police force for his second son, there was doubt as to whether or not Hector's uncertain health would hold up under the rigors of tropical service. There was but one way to find out: in the early summer of 1893 Hector was sent to Burma.

The outward voyage must have been absorbing for a youth of Munro's adventurous nature and writer's proclivities; but, when he at last arrived in Burma, the land of his birth, he may have felt a mixture of fascination and repulsion for its vile greenness, its heat, its filth, its stench, its noise of thrusting humanity. Brother Charles, who met him at the dock in Rangoon, helped him settle into the strange, new life. Hector was given a commissioned rank which seems to have been the police equivalent of a lieutenant; his detail of policemen, or "guards," were all Burmese.

Hector, after being briefed on his duties, was assigned to a tour of police posts scattered in various towns and villages around the Mandalay district. In the discharge of his duties, he traveled about on horseback and in bullock carts with his "guard" of sturdy, cheerful little brown men. Often, this life was a wild and primitive one for a young man who had been reared in genteel circumstances; he traveled through jungle, along the rice-paddied banks of wild rivers, over difficult terrain. One of his own drawings, which he sent home to show his people what his Burmese life was like, is captioned "Tobogganning in the Shan Hills." It shows three policemen leading their horses down the precarious footing of a steep slope, preceded in the wilderness by three buffaloes which are bearing massive panniers containing the party's supplies while crossing a stream. It is impossible to tell which of the men Munro represented as himself, although the man in the center of the picture brandishes a rifle held at the balance. Nothing could emphasize more than this drawing the contrast between his former leisured life in England and the sweaty, masculine exertions necessary to police the Empire.

Munro's experiences with the commonplaces of crime—assault, murder, housebreaking, thievery, the many Eastern forms of prostitution—are carefully excluded from his published work; it would have been "bad form" to write about them. These deeds confirmed Munro's cynicism about human nature, although he never criticized the theory and practice of imperialism. Inevitably, the contrast comes to mind between the gradual humanization and liberalization of George Orwell, when he too served as a policeman in Burma a generation later, and Munro's uncompromisingly imperial views. Orwell was gradually disenchanted with the imperial system, but to expect any criticism of it from Munro would be futile. The colonial servant of Munro's day simply ignored any unfairness or severity of the British Raj. Munro might criticize a colonial career for being a boring, futile way of life, as he did in *The Unbearable Bassington;* but to attack the system's rationale would have been a crime viler than mutiny or *lèse-majesté*.

This Burmese interval had relatively little effect upon Munro's literary efforts; perhaps he felt that Rudyard Kipling had worked the vein of the British observer in an Eastern colony for about all it was worth, although material from the Burmese experience does appear now and again in his work. In May, 1914, Munro wrote in a "Potted Parliament" dispatch: "It used to be required of me once that I should ride about the highways and byways of Mandalay at dead of night, visiting sleepy police patrols, and I almost invariably had a pack of native dogs yelping and demonstrating at my pony's heels. . . . I missed them dreadfully if private feuds or some other business drew them off in some other direction."[18]

In his essay "The Comments of Moung Ka" Munro recalled the people and countryside of Burma:

> On two sides of the house there was a bright-green swamp, which stretched away to where uncultivated jungle growth began. In the bright-green swamp, which was really a rice-field when you looked closely at it, bitterns and pond-herons and elegant cattle egrets stalked and peered with the absorbed air of careful and conscientious reptile hunters. . . . In the tall reed growth by the riverside grazing buffaloes showed in patches of dark slaty blue . . . and in the tamarind trees that shaded Moung Ka's house the crows . . . kept up their incessant afternoon din. . . . Moung Ka sat smoking his enormous green-brown cigar, without which no Burmese man, woman or child seems really complete. . . . His friend Moung Thwa, dealer in teakwood, had just returned down-river from distant Bhamo, where he had spent many weeks in dignified, unhurried chaffering with Chinese merchants.[19]

And the boredom of Munro, the erstwhile London sophisticate, may be inferred from this passage in *The Unbearable Bassington:*

> He would be in some unheard-of sun-blistered wilderness, where natives and pariah dogs and raucous-throated crows fringed round

mockingly on one's loneliness, where one rode for sweltering miles for the chance of meeting a collector or police officer, with whom most likely on closer acquaintance one had hardly two ideas in common, where female society was represented at long intervals by some climate-withered woman missionary or official's wife, where food and sickness and veterinary lore became at last the three outstanding subjects on which the mind settled or rather sank.[20]

But Munro never allowed any sign of this unpleasantness to show in his letters to his family. Ethel published in her biography excerpts from fifteen of Munro's letters from Burma;[21] everywhere through these letters is the foreshadowing of his writer's gifts. The letters display a worldliness and sophistication remarkable in a man in his early twenties. They reflect a broad general knowledge, a highly individual sense of humor, and a peppering of biblical and other religious references which reflect the enforced piety of the Broadgate years.

It is in the fluency of the writing, the observation, the vivid invention, the originality of phrasing that these missives exhibit the talents of the born writer. Munro's Swedish translator, John Karlzen, published these letters from Burma as a supplement to Ethel's biography rather than as an integral section of it.[22] Karlzen showed shrewdness in presenting them in this fashion; the letters from Burma are really Munro's first literary creations.

Munro performed satisfactorily enough as a policeman, executing his duties conscientiously and bearing the heat, the discomforts, the boredom, and the fevers with stoicism. It would have been in a long family tradition had he succeeded in making a career as a colonial servant; but, as it turned out, English literature was the eventual winner. Ethel wrote that "Hector was in Burma only thirteen months and had seven fevers in that time. . . . In the summer months Hector got malaria very badly, and in August had to resign and come home." [23] His physique had not been tough enough to sustain the hard test of empire building in the tropics.

CHAPTER 2

The Unaccepted Historian

MUNRO'S father went to London to meet him when he landed, and he found him in such bad physical condition that he immediately put Munro under a nurse's care. When the son was strong enough to travel again, the father took him back to Devonshire, to the new home of the little family at Buckleigh, above the cliffs at Westward Ho!, where Munro began a long, slow convalescence. The climate of Devonshire was a healthy contrast to the mugginess of the tropics, and many British soldiers and civil servants who had spent their careers in India and in other infernos of the Empire retired to the area for this reason. Once again it is difficult to feel sorry for Munro; he made his convalescence in surroundings so comfortable and solicitous that they would not have been the lot of most other invalids.

Ethel wrote of "our coachman" and "our housemaid" at Buckleigh, and Munro made the unconcerned purchase of a horse on which to join the local hunt. And he wrote later of "the cool grey skies and wet turf and moist ploughlands of an English hunting country." [1] The ordeal of his convalescence is apparent, however, in Munro's treatment of Yeovil, the "hero" of *When William Came:* "He was desperately tired after his day's hunting, a legacy of weakness that the fever had bequeathed to him . . . he could scarcely sit upright in his saddle. . . . His foreign travels, his illness, his recent weeks in London . . . had very slight and distant connexion with his present existence." [2]

During his convalescence, Munro had the opportunity to observe clinically the upper-middle-class people of the "county" families about whom he was to write so frequently and knowledgeably. He profited even more, during this period of enforced leisure, from his reacquaintance with the strange, haunting Devon countryside and with the ordinary, working-class people of Devon.[3] Although it is one of the loveliest counties of England,

Devonshire is also one of the counties most hagridden by a spooky folklore. It is lush country, but its topography is largely a chaotic series of hills and valleys: the famous combes, with farms worked into the hillside; the very name Devon is from the Celtic "Dyfnaint," a place of "dark and deep valleys."

The dark spirits of Devonshire seeped into Munro's soul, and he absorbed, perhaps subconsciously, the superstitions and the ghostly folklore all around him. Here is unquestionably the source of the deep and abiding interest in the supernatural which so frequently appears in Munro's fiction.

I *To Be a Writer*

His sister Ethel's biography, the only source book about Munro's life and aspirations, deals with Munro's decision to become a professional writer with the imperceptive and uninformative words, "In 1896, Hector left for London, to earn his living by writing . . . he wrote naturally and never went through a correspondence course."[4]

Only a strong sense of duty and family tradition had forced Munro to attempt a colonial career of thirty or forty years in a cul-de-sac, in the antipathetic company of the bureaucrats and Colonel Blimps who administered the Empire. Now that his illnesses had eliminated a colonial career, he could attempt the storming of the literary citadels where he felt instinctively that there was a foreordained place for him.

As a first step he took lodgings at 97 Mortimer Street in London, occasionally varying this urban life with brief trips back to his family in North Devon. The convention of the aspiring young writer starving in a garret while he struggles to gain a handhold in literature certainly did not apply to Munro. Apparently he had some money of his own to live on, supplemented by family contributions during these unremunerative first years. And Munro, the son of a colonel and the grandson of an admiral, with the requisite social polish, background, and breeding must have had many invitations to dine out in town houses and to weekend at country places.

With a determination and a self-discipline that were native qualities, Munro set to work on the composition of a history of medieval Russia. To be a historian had a cachet about it of being a moneyed amateur, and thus it would be a most acceptable pursuit to the right people. Those other avenues open to a beginning writer, journalism and the writing of short fiction were, in Munro's time and class, considered vulgar and faintly disreputable.

This, his first book, *The Rise of the Russian Empire,* was a rather heavy undertaking. Ethel wrote that "he spent much time in the British Museum Reading Room getting material for his book." [5] His research necessitated his reading Russian in the original; somewhere during his earlier life he had learned Russian with its added barrier of a Cyrillic alphabet, probably during the years of permissive study at Heanton. There is a very noticeably Russian thread in Munro's life; for, first of all, he spent two years in St. Petersburg as correspondent to the London *Morning Post,* a most particular paper whose reporters had to be knowledgeable and expert in their places of assignment. This long St. Petersburg service was a testimony to Munro's insight into the Russian soul and to his sympathy for the Russian people's struggle to lift themselves into the modern world. After Munro's return from Russia, he helped welcome the first visit of the Russian Ballet troupe to England, and there are Russian characters and references to Russia scattered through his later fiction.

In *The Rise of the Russian Empire* Munro, the medievalist and dilettante in heraldry and genealogy, had chosen a subject and a historical period which were most congenial. Munro stated his intention in the Preface to this book:

> With the exception of a translation of Rambaud's somewhat disjointed work, there is no detailed history of Russia in the English language at all approaching modern standards. The reigns of Peter the Great and of some of his successors down to the present day—a period covering only 200 years—have been minutely dealt with, but the earlier history of a nation with whom we are coming ever closer into contact is to the English reader almost a blank. Whether the work now submitted will adequately fill the gap remains to be seen; such is its object.[6]

The Rise of the Russian Empire, a book of eighty thousand words in its eleven chapters, traces the history of European Russia from the middle of the ninth century to 1619. The work begins with Munro's imagined picture of the vast Russian land in the time of prehistory, and then he discusses the consequences to Europe of the breakup of the Holy Roman Empire; the Scandinavian invasion of northern Russia and subsequent attacks upon Byzantium; the conversion of many Russians to Christianity in the tenth century; the bloody dynastic feuds of the twelfth and thirteenth centuries; the conquest of European Russia by the Mongols, with its lingering malaise; the conquest by the Teutons of western Russia and its subsequent liberation by Slavs at the Battle of Tannenberg; the rise of Muscovy to the hegemony of the other Russian city-states; the unifying figure of Ivan the Terrible; the regency and later coronation of a figure famous in grand opera, Boris Godounov; the rejection of the pretender, the "False Dmitri"; and finally, the emergence of the modern era under the Romanov dynasty.

The principal fault of *The Rise of the Russian Empire* is the confusion it engenders in the general reader. The book's subject and its material are much too involved and full of incident to be compressed efficiently in the limits of a three-hundred-page book. Munro himself has given a description of this incoherence which may be applied from the specific incident he mentions to the whole book: "The history of Russia during the next two hundred years is little more than a chronicle of aimless and inconsequent feuds between the multiple Princes of the Blood—the 'much-too-many' of their crowded little world—overlaid and beclouded with strange-sounding names recurring and clashing in a luxuriant tangle of pedigree, and further embarrassed by a perpetual shifting and reshifting of the family appanages." [7]

At many points in the book Munro's style becomes lush and purple, a manner not at all typical of the later cool detachment of his fiction. Apparently, he was often carried away by the bloody, clashing pageantry of his subject. Indeed, the impression Munro leaves today is one of attempting to infuse life and color, by an art similar to the novelist's, into the hitherto dry and colorless writing of most history books. For his pains in attempting this innovation, he won the enmity of some of the professional historians. The color and pageantry which the Russian motion picture director Sergei Eisenstein managed to impart beneath the obligatory propaganda in his films *Alexander Nevsky* and *Ivan the Terrible* would certainly have delighted Munro; these are just the effect he was trying to achieve.

The Rise of the Russian Empire presaged, however, many of Munro's writing characteristics. Munro as a writer had, for example, the ability to project his conceptions of people and places into the reader's imagination with extreme vividness. For example, there is the description of the Moscow of about 1510:

> Hemmed in on all sides with thick forests, from whence down the Moskva river was floated the timber of which the houses were mostly built, the city stood in a setting of open meadows, swarming with hare and roebuck, which were preserved for the Grand Prince's exclusive hunting. Fields and gardens and monasteries straggled so far into the outskirts (or slobodas) that it was difficult to tell exactly where the line of demarcation lay. . . . The Kreml, or citadel, and . . . the inner quarters of the town, were however strongly fortified. As is frequently the case in cities with Oriental characteristics, squalor and magnificence were strangely jumbled together. Mean huts and booths were interspersed with cupola-crowned churches and public buildings, which, designed for the most part by Byzantine and Italian artists, presented a quaint and not unpleasing confusion of eastern and western architecture. . . . Here, then, in this straggling wood-built metropolis, this germ-cell of the Russian Empire . . . amid a surrounding of cathedrals and mud, holy ikons and squalid hovels, dedicated gates and buildings topped with quaint bulbous domes and cupolas, gold, blue and silver, moved the rulers of the Moskovite state.[8]

Many of the figures of speech in *The Rise of the Russian Empire* have the instantly recognizable Munrovian flavor and originality, with a predominant imagery of Russian princes, peasants, and invaders as wild birds and feral beasts:

> Kiev . . . passed into the keeping of one prince after another, like a dainty piece of carrion dropped and snatched and fought over by a parcel of kites or crows.[9]
>
> As an advancing tide, engulfing in its progression the stretches of ooze-land which lie in its onward path sends scurrying before it flights of waders and other shore-haunting birds . . . so the great Mongol wave . . . drove before it disordered troops of the Polovtzi nomads.[10]
>
> Like unscathed pheasants stealing back one by one to the coverts from which the beaters had sent them whirring forth, the fugitive princes returned to the wrecks of their provinces.[11]
>
> Like a dog of too accommodating disposition, he wagged his tail to whichever master shouted loudest.[12]

• • •

Not so lightly were they to be rid of these dusky, wolf-eyed warriors, who teemed in the wide, arid plain-land of Asia like rats on an old threshing-floor.[13]

Munro's preoccupation with the cruelty of the human animal is apparent all through the book:

Some petitioners from Pskov, upon whom was poured blazing spirits, which ignited their hair, beards and clothes.[14]

Ivan . . . drove his iron-tipped staff through the foot of the messenger and kept it there while he read it; and it was a long letter.[15]

Kniaz Dimitri Shaverov expiated his real or imputed crimes by a slow death by impalement. All day long, it was said, he lingered, bearing his pain heroically.[16]

Munro, in his treatment of religion in the book, took a most patronizing and superior stand. He never bothered to conceal his contempt of all the religions, both formal and unsophisticated, with which he had to deal in the book. Obviously an agnostic himself, he belittled the varieties of religious experience with an insouciance that must have infuriated the conventional and upright among his readers. All through his book Munro seems to be asking, "What will the blighters believe in next?" As an instance of how he amused himself, there is an exposition of how Vladimir, in the tenth century, came to choose the Eastern rite of Christianity, which has so estranged Russia from Western Europe:

In no country was the transition from paganism effected in so remarkable manner as in Russia. Vladimir, who had shown much zeal in erecting and ornamenting statues of Peroun at Kiev and Novogrod, grew suddenly dissatisfied with the national worship. . . . While contemplating a desertion of the old religion he naturally wished to replace it with the most reliable form of faith obtainable, and for this purpose trusty counsellors were sent on a mission of inquiry to Rome, to Constantinople, to the Volga-Bulgarians (who had embraced Islam), and to the Jews. . . . When the scattered envoys returned, the result of their investigations was laid before Vladimir, and this young man in search of a religion examined and compared the pretensions of the competing creeds. . . . The splendid ceremonial of the Greek Church, particularly in the service of S. Sophia at Constantinople. . . . The recital of these splendours inclined the Prince to a favourable consideration of the Greek faith, if indeed he had not previously had leanings towards that religion. . . . "If the Greek religion had not been the true religion, would your grandmother Olga, the wisest of mortals, have adopted it?" asked the partisans of the new doctrine; and the matter was settled. . . . The conversion of the people followed in due course; the wooden statue of Peroun, with its silver face and moustache of gold, was thrown down, flogged with whips, and hurled into the Dnieper, whose water cast it up again on the bank. The affrighted people rushed to worship their old god, but the Prince's men pushed him back into the current, and Peroun the silver-faced was swept down the stream and vanished. . . . On the banks of the same river that had engulfed their fallen idol the inhabitants of Kiev were mustered by command, and after the Greek priests had consecrated its waters, into it at a given signal plunged the whole wondering multitude, men, women, and children, and were baptized in one batch. A like scene was enacted at Novgorod, with the substitution of the Volkhov for the Dnieper, and throughout Russia the transition was effected in an equally successful manner. . . . The adoption of Christianity in its Greek form exercised a momentous influence on the history of Russia.[17]

One simply did not write in 1900, in this fashion, about religion and the religious instinct. The subject had to be treated with the utmost solemnity and with respect for dogmas and beliefs. Munro must have realized this, but the plain conclusion is that he did not give a damn about ruffling the feathers of the piously orthodox. The attitude throughout the book of skepticism not only toward formal religion but toward the pomposity of historians in general anticipated the "de-bunking" school of historians which arose like an undigested gorge in the 1920's. Munro composed his first book with much the same approach and intent that Lytton Strachey wielded to break a number of overrevered ikons twenty-odd years later.

Obvious also throughout the book is Munro's natural combativeness. He never wrote deprecatingly of the wastefulness of battles and wars, although he invariably wrote with contempt of the compromiser and the advocate of "peace at any price"—a revelation of Munro's own pugnacity. Lord Charnwood was to write of Munro's martial proclivities: "The fighting blood in him was hotter than in most men." [18]

There is no indication that Munro's book was commissioned beforehand; more than likely the manuscript was hawked around various publishers' offices. The book was published in 1900 by

Grant Richards, a gambler on new writers, who seemed to divine the well of talent in Munro. Richards, in fact, was even more than a gambler: he was a plunger, because he went into bankruptcy more than once. Yet the publication of *The Rise of the Russian Empire* seemed to have made no impression upon Richards, because in his own two volumes of reminiscences he failed to mention either Munro or his Russian book.

The book was not a financial success, and the reading public did not react with any enthusiasm to this rigorously original writer. And critically, the book's reception was mixed. Publications with an unspecialized readership were quite kind; typical of this sort of review was the one that appeared in *The Bookman:*

> Mr. Hector Munro has made a courageous and intelligent effort . . . to give the English people some notion of the tangled web of early Russian history. . . . Mr. Munro has succeeded very well in spinning the main threads of his subjects so as to make the English reader realise Russia's evolution from a vast conglomerate of distracted, foe-ridden, sundered territories into a coherent empire. . . . it is something of a feat to have so straightened out, proportioned, and abbreviated the intermingling mazes of Muscovite fortunes through these dark ages.[19]

The professional historians, however, were by and large quite hostile to Munro's contribution. Typical of their negative reaction was the review by Professor Archibald Carey Coolidge:

> In these days . . . a clear account of the early history and development of this mighty state should appeal to the general public as well as to the scholar . . . the task was tempting and not too difficult. How has it been fulfilled in the present volume? . . . A lack of broader knowledge . . . is shown by Mr. Munro's old-fashioned view of the Byzantine Empire, now rejected by all students of the subject, and by his treatment of Polish topics and his spelling of Polish names, and by his repetition of the usual exaggerations as to the size of the Tartar armies. When he attempts parallels, they are not particularly happy; witness his comparison between Oleg and Charlemagne, which is absurd. Still, it is not with the detail of his facts, in the main accurate enough, that we have to quarrel with him; it is rather in his appreciation and treatment of them. Not merely is he prejudiced, as when his dislike to the Orthodox church—and it would seem to the Christian faith in general—makes him entirely fail to grasp how

much their religion and its ministers have done for the Russian people; he has also fallen, and fallen helplessly, into the commonest of all mistakes in dealing with things Russian, that of regarding them as abnormal. Thus, instead of treating the early history as a subject, interesting and in some ways peculiar enough, but still perfectly comprehensible, and fundamentally governed by the same rules as that of other states, he is continually trying to impress us with the strangeness of his theme. There is a striving for effect from the beginning to the end of the book; nothing is ever natural, it is all lurid or grotesque or both. The result of this craving for the picturesque is a confused mass of word painting, which only a brilliant style could have redeemed; and the style is atrocious . . . there is no excuse for the badness of pages of turgid rhetoric mixed with ineffective sarcasms, not infrequently in bad taste. . . . These faults would deserve less attention if they were defects in English. Unfortunately they are characteristic of Mr. Munro's whole attitude toward his subject and indicate his failure as an historian . . . the unnecessary parade of accuracy (in place names) seems like part of the general striving of effect which is the chief cause of the disappointment one feels in reading what might otherwise have been a useful book.[20]

Although rebuffed in his effort to join the jealous little circle of the professional historians, Munro curiously enough agreed with them that his book was not a particularly brilliant effort; Ethel wrote that "Hector himself had not a great opinion of the book." [21] As might be expected, Munro's first book disappeared in the same unobtrusive manner in which it was born. Long out of print, it never appears in the bibliographies of Russian histories written in the present day, possibly because modern historians do not know of its existence. Certainly, it is startlingly different from the other things about which Munro wrote.

CHAPTER 3

The Journalist Perforce

WITH the publication of *The Rise of the Russian Empire,* Munro could at last with justification consider himself a writer. He had negotiated the chasm which separates the unfledged amateur from the published author, and his book was on the tables of booksellers, on the shelves of discriminating readers, and in the card catalogues of great libraries. Nevertheless, it was evident that Munro could not achieve self-support by writing books and that, if he was serious about his intent to earn his livelihood as a writer, he would have to descend to the vulgar journalistic struggle in Fleet Street. J. W. Lambert wrote of this moment of truth:

> Young Munro, once out of the British Museum Reading Room, set about earning a little money by writing very short stories for newspapers and magazines. How he fared it is impossible to say; but one of these exercises found itself in print in 1899. A story called "Dogged" appeared in a periodical called *St. Paul's*. . . . The story, which appears over the initials H. H. M., is labouriously facetious but announces several of Saki's favourite themes. Its hero is a dull and meek young man, its anti-hero a spirited dog, by whose means a blameless life is insensibly turned into one of idleness and dissipation.[1]

Munro's sister described the ending of this time of floundering: "Some Devon friends introduced him to Sir Francis Gould (then Carruthers Gould), who launched him in the literary world."[2] Munro was fortunate indeed to be chosen as a protégé by Gould, who was the celebrated political cartoonist of the *Westminster Gazette;* from his long journalistic experience he recognized that Munro's natural acerbity was well suited to the writing of political satire. And the London newspapers of that day afforded the most receptive testing ground for new writers. A. A. Milne wrote of this arena of opportunity, "Let us spare a moment, and a tear, for those golden days in the early nineteen hundreds, when there were five leisurely papers of an evening in which the free-lance might graduate." [3]

In the early summer of 1900 Gould and Munro sought an audience with J. A. Spender, the editor of the *Westminster Gazette*, and Spender himself later described that meeting:

> I have a clear recollection of Gould's bringing him to my room at the office . . . and starting then and there on a discussion of articles which the one was to write and the other to illustrate. "Saki" left most of the talking to Gould, and at the beginning one had to dig hard to get a word out of him. But the word when it came was pungent and original, and in a few minutes I came to the conclusion that Gould was justified in his "find." The scheme suggested was that of the *Westminster Alice*—dealing with the South African war and politics in general . . . and I own that I had misgivings about it. Parodies of the famous original had several times been submitted (as I suppose to most editors) and nearly all had been dismal failures. . . . I cannot imagine anyone doubting that "Saki" is one of the few who have succeeded. . . . Gould catches the spirit of Tenniel, though in his own rougher manner, with the same felicity as "Saki" does that of Lewis Carroll. I well remember the pleasure of both in this collaboration and their long consultations before the result was produced.[4]

The odd thing about the partnership was that politically Munro was a Conservative who was innately Tory in his outlook on the world, while Gould was a Liberal of the Radical degree. And the *Westminster Gazette* itself was thoroughly Liberal in its attitudes, so much so that it was considered to be the voice of the Liberal party. It made, however, no concessions to the ignorance and near-illiteracy of the masses. Immaculately written and edited, the *Westminster Gazette* was one of the few London papers a man could read without demeaning himself, as Bernard Shaw remarked; and Arnold Bennett made the habitual reading of this enlightened journal one of the integral parts of his admired short story, "The Death of Simon Fuge."

The fact that the *Westminster Gazette* accepted and published Munro's material, in spite of his innately reactionary views on the human condition, is evidence that the educated, Brahmin, intellectually fastidious element in Great Britain was not confined to either of the two great political parties of that day. The gentlemen of the Establishment, be they Liberal or Conservative, could understand "Saki's" references and appreciate his parallels. Besides, there was an air of "business is business" about the *Westminster's* purchase of the clever copy of the known Tory, Munro.

Munro could have found no more knowledgeable guide than Gould to initiate him into the workaday atmosphere of Fleet Street by introducing him to the personalities of that inky world. And Gould was a "quick study" in apprehending what his writers and editors wanted in his drawings to point up what they were trying to impart in their prose; although he was admittedly a very ordinary draftsman, largely self-taught in drawing, he had a gift for capturing excellent likenesses of his victims.

Munro chose the pen name "Saki" for his part of the collaboration. Saki was the cupbearer to the gods in the *Rubáiyát of Omar Khayyam.*[5]

I *The Beginning of the "Saki" Reputation*

Eleven of the *Westminster Alice* pieces are reprinted in book form, presented in the order in which they were written, "with apologies to Sir John Tenniel and to everybody else concerned." These sketches enlarged upon some of the more ludicrous events of the British political scene, besides making diversionary attacks on such targets as the established religion in Great Britain and the incomprehensibility of Poet Laureate, Alfred Austin. Because of their consistent exposure of the government's mishandling of the Boer War, they became an eagerly anticipated feature of the *Westminster.*

The Boer War had lost its original hysterical popularity in Britain and was now undergoing a phase of unpopularity because of the disparity in size of the antagonists, and the incompetence ("ineptitude") with which it was conducted by the British. The analogy of the American Civil War is rather pertinent: a population living close to the land, the Boers displayed an aptitude for militarism that far outshone the efforts of its larger, industrialized adversary, the British. Munro himself might reasonably have been expected to serve in the war—he was only thirty years old and his health was now much stronger—but he preferred to criticize it from London. Englishmen did not volunteer in the vast numbers with which they swamped the recruiting offices in 1914; the Boer War hadn't the appeal of World War I, possibly because most Britons felt that their country was cast in the bully's part.

When the first *Alice* piece appeared in the *Westminster Gazette* of July 15, 1900, the victim of Munro's harshest gibes was A. J. Balfour, the Tory government's First Lord of the Treasury. Balfour was represented as "the Ineptitude," drawn as an auk, his bird's body curved into the attitude of languor which Balfour brought to debates in the House of Commons; this satire was cruelly accurate. The government in power at that time was Conservative, Munro's own persuasion; but its political identity did not prevent Munro from attacking it for incompetence and stupidity.

Another piece, "Alice in Pall Mall," continued the theme of the government's mishandling of the Boer War. The Secretary of State for War, the Marquess of Lansdowne, had just been promoted to the post of Foreign Secretary to rid the government of his embarrassing incompetence. Lord Lansdowne is represented as the White Knight who changed horses from the War Office to the Foreign Office with the smugness that was typical of the dunderheaded element of the upper classes:

> "You see, I had read a book" said the Knight "Written to prove that warfare under modern conditions was impossible. You may imagine how disturbing that was to a man of my profession. . . . You will never guess what I did." Alice pondered. "You went to war of course—" "Yes; *but not under modern conditions.*" The Knight stopped his horse. . . . "Now, for instance," he continued kindly, seeing that Alice had not recovered her breath, "You observe this little short-range gun that I have hanging on my saddle? Why do you suppose that I have sent out guns of that particular kind? Because, if they happened to fall into the hands of the enemy, they'd be very little use to him. That was my own invention." [6]

J. A. Spender noted that this piece was one of the most successful of Munro's thrusts in the series: "Of the many political squibs I can remember none had so immediate and complete a success as this. It was quoted everywhere, and the whole town joined in the laugh." [7] But, by the words "the whole town," Spender meant the influential men of London—the politicians, the clubmen, the powerful and wealthy. Munro had been accepted by the elect audience for which he had searched. Spender continued:

> The first section belongs to July, 1900, and reflects the general uneasiness at the continuance of the Boer War. . . . It had been a moot point since the war broke out whether the public was angrier with the Boers, the pro-Boers or the Government. . . . Mr. Balfour . . . had got labelled as the "philosophic doubter" and the phrase summed up all that the public found most irritating in the attitude of the Government, its air of being the victim of circumstances which no wisdom could have been expected to foresee.[8]

Once in a while criticisms of the conduct of the war changed in the series to scoffing examinations of other currently newsworthy topics. In the piece "Alice at Lambeth" Munro explored the dissatisfaction in Parliament with the Roman Catholic characteristics of the Church of England, the state religion. The Church's head, the Archbishop of Canterbury, is represented as the Duchess in a parody of the scene in the pepper-laden kitchen. "There was a faint whiff of burning incense," Munro interpolated, "and some candles that had just been put out were smouldering unpleasantly." The Duchess underwent a pepper-pot attack by the cook whose features were plainly identifiable as those of a militantly Protestant Member of Parliament. When the Cheshire Cat suddenly appeared and asked about the disappearance of the baby, Alice replied "It went out—to roam, I think." [9]

Hunting for smaller game, the team of Gould and Munro chose as a target the Poet Laureate, Alfred Austin, who was not guilty of ineffectual leadership or political indifference, but of perpetrating ineffable poesy. In "Alice In a Fog" Gould depicted Austin as the White Rabbit hurrying off to present his poetic work on the return of the future King George V and his wife from a state visit to Australia. Munro attempted, to no effect, to analyze several of Austin's poetic lines: " 'It seems to be a kind of poetry' said Alice doubtfully; 'At least,' she added, 'some of the words rhyme and none of them appear to have any meaning. . . . I'll give sixpence to any one who can explain it.' " [10]

In "Alice Lunches at Westminster" Munro returned to the Boer War and considered the case of a general who had been whitewashed for his incompetence in South Africa and, like Lord Lansdowne, was actually retained by the government in another capacity. General Sir Redvers Buller, V. C., made an effort in a rather incoherent speech in the Queen's Hall, Westminster, to defend his new appointment. Gould drew Buller as a uniformed Humpty Dumpty on a wall, and he looked remarkably like the Colonel Blimp of later British history. Buller denied advising the besieged city of Ladysmith to surrender to the Boers, and here there was a fortuitous parallel with the original Lewis Carroll, who put rhyming lines of an extreme incomprehensibility into the mouth of Humpty Dumpty. Munro had only to transpose Buller's incoherent account of his own conduct before Ladysmith into cryptic doggerel to achieve a telling indictment of the British military leadership. The fact that Buller, like Munro, was an Old Boy from Pencarwick school did not soften Munro's satire.

As a series, the *Westminster Alice* enjoyed a *succès d'estime* with the small but select, informed audience at which Munro was aiming. Although Gould's drawings are apt and Tennielesque, it is Munro's prose that is the more skillfully adapted to capturing the spirit of Lewis Carroll. J. A. Spender confirmed this ability: "Such things must either succeed perfectly or fail lamentably, and to succeed perfectly meant not merely copying the form but catching the spirit of the inimitable fantastic original." And Spender then added, significantly, "I cannot imagine any one doubting that 'Saki' is one of the few who have succeeded." [11]

In March, 1902, the *Westminster Gazette* published the *Westminster Alice* series in book form, with soft covers, at a price of sixpence. The little book was such a success that the newspaper republished it in hard covers the following June at a price of two and six. Munro's journalistic debut had been a solid if limited success.[12]

Besides giving a picture of the political figures and events in turn-of-the-century Britain, a setting which now seems so unshakable and secure, the *Westminster Alice* was the first evidence of Munro's deep interest in the politics of England and of the various European countries in which he was to live. His preoccupation with watching and recording the actions of politicians in their natural habitats, the parliaments of Europe, is yet another but little-known aspect of Munro as a writer.

About this time Munro suffered another very serious illness. Ethel wrote: "Somewhere before 1902 Hector had a severe attack of double pneumonia in London. After his recovery he seemed to be much stronger than he had ever been before and continued so for the rest of his life." [13] Strength of will, which was such a big part of Munro's character, never appeared so forcefully as when he had to summon it to combat some deathly illness.

II *"The Political Jungle-Book"*

In an apparent effort to capitalize on the success of the *Westminster Alice* pieces, Gould and Munro collaborated on a second venture for the *Westminster Gazette.* Between February and November of 1902 they chose Rudyard Kipling as a model for their continuing parodies of Parliamentary shenanigans. The immensely popular Rudyard Kipling had recently published his *Just So Stories,* in which various animals and birds of the Indian jungle speak with human tongue. Kipling himself had drawn, rather crudely, the original illustrations for the *Just So Stories,* so that it was not too difficult for Gould to invest Kipling's animal creations with the faces of currently active British politicians—Joseph Chamberlain, Lord Rosebery, Balfour (who appeared as "Sheer Khan't, the tiger"), Asquith, Hugh Cecil, Morley, and Munro's own *bête noire,* Lloyd George.

Seven of these pieces appeared in a series whose title changed about halfway through from the "Not So Stories" to "The Political Jungle-Book." The choice of Kipling as a peg on which to hang their whips was not nearly so felicitous as their first model, Lewis Carroll; and the "Not So" series failed to impart any magic. Moreover, a modern reader lacks the invaluable identifications of personalities by J. A. Spender to guide him through the maze of British politics in 1902. Even Gould's drawings, which now betray a certain crudeness, do not blend too well with Munro's text. Very obviously, this vein of derivative satire was now worked out.

There is a rather detailed memoir of Munro during this first London period at the turn of the century. It was written by Munro's first cousin Cecil William Mercer, who was then a schoolboy, and who in later life was a prolific novelist under the pseudonym of Dornford Yates. Mercer wrote in part that "Hector had beautiful manners, talked easily and well. . . . He was thirty or thirty-one—a spare man of average height, brown-eyed, clean-shaven, with a ready smile and a most intelligent face. His hands were sensitive, and he kept them very still. His complexion was sallow. He was well-groomed and neat in his attire. Always wore a bowler in London. Never careless or untidy in his dress." [14]

By reading between the lines of "Dornford Yates's" memoir, it may be inferred that Munro, with his gentleman's attitudes and his strivings for the elegant life still had not accepted the realities of journalism and the journalist's life. Munro yet retained his original idea that there was something faintly disreputable about practicing journalism, that it was an unsuitable and undignified way of getting a living, like retail trade. He eventually abandoned his attitude of superiority and became a model of professionalism and dependability, a sort of editor's dream; but one may be sure that his entry into Fleet Street was full of misgivings.

III *The First of the Gilded Youth Portraits:* Reginald

In 1894 the *Westminster Gazette* had published a series of skits by Anthony Hope (Hawkins), the future creator of *The Prisoner of Zenda,* skits whose appeal had been directed toward the paper's enlightened, sophisticated readers. This series, *The Dolly Dialogues,* is a portrait of upper-class London as seen through the eyes of Dolly, a wealthy, privileged, but rather frivolous and fickle girl of that class. The narrator of the series, a self-effacing male, relays the amusing observations of Dolly about this fine upper world, observations whose superficiality are occasionally lighted by a piercing shrewdness.

The Westminster's editors may have discerned in Munro's talents a chance to repeat the earlier success of *The Dolly Dialogues,* or perhaps Munro himself suggested the creation of a series of irreverent portraits of London's Best People. At any rate, the *Westminster Gazette* published Munro's *Reginald* series throughout 1903 to a growing following of appreciative and delighted readers. In fifteen of these sketches Munro commented in an unflattering but highly amusing manner on the well-fed, well-heeled, but not always mentally well-endowed denizens of the British upper world. Ethel wrote of *Reginald:* "The characters in the stories are all imaginary. Reginald is a type composed of several young men, studied during his years of town life; Hector told me that more than one of his acquaintances considered himself the original." [15]

The *Reginald* stories are the fruit of Munro's observation and judgment of the wealthy, idle, self-indulgent people among whom he spent so much of his time during that period when he was composing *The Rise of the Russian Empire* and seeking a place in the indifferent sphere of London journalism. But, unlike *The Dolly Dialogues,* the *Reginald* sketches have no connecting line of a continuous plot. Munro relied on his inimitable wit and unconventional viewpoint in exploring the world of Society to make his readers anticipate Reginald's next appearance in the green pages of the *Westminster Gazette.* Imparting wittiness to Reginald was only natural for Munro: he himself was a brilliant conversationalist. Munro was, wrote Maurice Baring, "irresistibly witty and droll sometimes, sometimes ecstatically silly, so that he almost made you cry for laughter."[16]

Munro was ever able to transfer this funniness in conversation to his writing, so that the *Reginald* pieces read like the eavesdropping of a third party on the remarks of a highly amusing and irreverent *flâneur.* Here are Munro's thrifty retrievings of the double-edged aphorisms, the unexpected reversals of platitudes, the paradoxes and floutings of sacred convention which prodigally flavored his own conversation. In form, the *Reginald* sketches are straight third-person narratives turning into dialogues between Reginald and his nameless interlocutor, another gilded society youth, or between Reginald and the exalted personage of a Duchess.[17] The stories deal with aspects of the upper-class British way of life of that period: garden parties, the ritual viewing in art galleries, dining out in the great houses or in plush restaurants, theatergoing, and week-ending in the country.

Reginald is an extremely quotable book: it is, in fact, so thick-sewn with *mots* that the critic of Munro's writing is hard put to choose among those that best record the feel, look, and flavor of life in Britain's upper classes circa 1900:

From "Reginald" Why are women so fond of raking up the past? They're as bad as tailors, who invariably remember what you owe them for a suit long after you've ceased to wear it.[18]

From "Reginald on Christmas Presents" . . . the female relative . . . who "knows a tie is always useful" and sends you some spotted horror that you could only wear in secret or in Tottenham Court Road. It *might* have been useful had she kept it to tie up currant bushes with, when it would have served the double purpose of supporting the branches and frightening away the birds.[19]

From "Reginald on the Academy" To be clever in the afternoon argues that one is dining nowhere in the evening. . . . I hate posterity—it's so fond of having the last word.[20]

From "Reginald at the Theatre" Reginald waited for a couple of minutes while the Lord of Rimini temporarily monopolized the accoustic possibilities of the theatre. "That is the worst of tragedy," he observed, "One can't always hear oneself talk." [21]

From "Reginald's Choir Treat" Reginald . . . came down late to breakfast, and nibbled toast, and said disrespectful things about the universe. The family ate porridge, and believed in everything, even the weather forecast.[22]

From "Reginald on Worries" There's Marion Dulciber, who *would* think she could play bridge . . . Still you couldn't call it a sudden calamity; *that* occurred when poor dear Marion was born. The doctors said at the time that she couldn't live more than a fortnight, and she's been trying ever since to see if she could. Women are so opinionated.[23]

From "Reginald on House-Parties" . . . just when I was trying my best to understand half the things I was saying, being asked . . . how many fowls she could keep in a run ten feet by six. . . . I told her whole crowds, as long as she kept the door shut . . . she brooded over it for the rest of the dinner.[24]

From "Reginald at the Carlton" Isn't there a Bishop or somebody who believes we shall meet all the animals we have known on earth in another world? How frightfully embarrassing to meet a whole shoal of whitebait you had last known at Prince's. I'm sure in my nervousness I should talk of nothing but lemons.[25]

From "Reginald's Christmas Revel" There was a Major Somebody who had shot things in Lapland, or somewhere of that sort. . . . he was continually giving us the details of what they measured from tip to tip, as though he thought we were going to make them warm underthings for the winter. . . . and then one day I quite modestly gave the dimensions of an okapi I had shot in the Lincolnshire fens. The Major turned a beautiful Tyrian scarlet (I remember thinking at the time that I should like my bathroom hung in that colour).[26]

And from "Reginald On Besetting Sins" there is the famous, much anthologized: "On a raw Wednesday morning, in a few ill-chosen words, she told the cook that she drank. . . . The cook was a good cook, as cooks go; and as cooks go she went." [27]

Some critics have felt that *Reginald* is the best work Munro ever did; indeed, when these sketches were first published, they seem to have had considerable influence upon contemporary university youth. John Gore, for example, wrote of this influence:

> I was an undergraduate at Oxford. . . . Among the nocturnal joys . . . were regular variety entertainments arranged and carried out by gifted amateurs, for the most part fellow undergraduates. . . . Four youths were the key men in the cast of our variety entertainment. Their names were Harry Tennant, Jack Gilliat, Christopher Stone and Bill Mercer. . . . The fourth-named relied for his effects on the writings of "Saki," which at that time were delighting readers of the old "Westminster Gazette." Mercer learned many of these sketches by heart—the "Reginald" series—and delivered them inimitably, and before long, we, his audience, learned them by heart from his performance and were only too ready to anticipate his coming rocket before the last had burst in a salvo of bright stars.[28]

Commentators on Munro's work usually make pyrotechnical comparisons and use shellburst similes when they write about *Reginald*. Gore continued: "We thought of him ['Saki'] as a contemporary, one Reginald, somewhat . . . of a 'Lounge-lizard,' a boy who cared too much for his personal appearance. . . . A rather unwholesome boy, we thought, with a taste for sweet liquers and Persian art, one who played no games, could not 'hit a hay-stack' and said disrespectful things about big-game hunters and Blimps. But we never questioned his wit, if we questioned his morals."[29]

Reginald's effete languor and *soigné* idleness seem to have caused a misconception of Munro's own person and character; for, as Hugh Walpole wrote,

> . . . a great many people spoke of them [the *Reginald* stories] as ephemera, the brilliant journalism of a rather light and butterfly character. In his own personality during these years he carried on this superstition; he was to be met at country houses and London parties apparently rather cynical, rather idle and taking life so gently that he might hardly be said to take it at all. Certain intimate friends of his knew that this was not the truth but they supported the disguise and encouraged it; it saved him, we cannot doubt, a number of tiresome obligations. . . . Then came the war. He, who had been the frivolous hero of drawing-rooms and Sunday afternoons

in the country, who seemed to consider no purpose in life more important than the production of a brilliant epigram, who might have laughed at patriotism as something too serious to be considered by any right-minded person, went instantly to the wars as a soldier in the ranks.[30]

The portrait of the upper-class England of that day which is drawn in the *Reginald* series is presented as being comically reprehensible. And yet not every line that Munro set down is heartless, flippant, or worldly, or in a style of writing concerned only with paradox and brittle wit. The usual commentaries on *Reginald* have given these sketches a reputation for lightheartedly reporting the foibles of the stuffed shirts and overupholstered *grande dames* of London society while they are written with a giddy unconcern for the inequities of the social system which permitted such abuses. Munro in *Reginald* was occasionally critical of some of the sacred institutions of the upper world, but he criticized so lightly that his readers seldom felt his sting. In "Reginald at the Theatre," for example, Munro made a few observations on "philanthropy" as practiced smugly by the upper classes. The Duchess brags to Reginald that, "whenever want or misery or starvation is known to exist, however distant or difficult of access, we instantly organize relief on the most generous scale. . . ." "'I wonder,' said Reginald, 'if you have ever walked down the Embankment on a winter night?'"[31]

There is no other interpretation of this sally but that Munro was here flicking at the obtuseness of a governing class that allowed such awful things to exist. Munro, through Reginald, was not always complacent when he wrote about the pomp and glittering surface of the great world. This "great world," as described in the *Reginald* sketches, was founded on exploitation, ignorance, and, above all, on widespread poverty. The misery of the lowest part of the human pyramid, whose apex is so vividly presented in *Reginald*, is almost unbelievable in this day and age. The homeless and the unemployed of the London of 1900 were condemned to a way of life of such misery and brutal squalor that an instant death would have seemed more desirable.

Jack London, in his youth and strength, and under the shield of his flaming spirit, lived in these lower depths of London for a while around the year 1901. He underwent this experience in order to gather material for a series of articles, and what he saw and felt is set down in his savage book *The People of the Abyss.* The condition of the very poor and the unemployed of London was certainly no cause for complacency in the governing classes. To Munro's credit, he recognized this horror, even if only for one passing mention in the *Reginald* series.

Munro was not attempting to create a three-dimensional character in Reginald; no one could possibly have been so consistently artificial and flippant as Munro made him. When one gets past the irreverence and parasitism, there is very little else to uncover in the shallow Reginald character. Reginald, though, is the first of the line of young male jokers and mischief-makers whom Munro created—the Clovises, Berties, Comuses. And, in creating Reginald, Munro pioneered in the exposition of a certain type of young man infesting the British upper classes, irresponsible and often scatterbrained.

P. G. Wodehouse, of course, is the best-known practitioner of writing about this sort of young man; but he did not pioneer the literary presentation of this type. Munro must be credited with making the first dissection of the species and with inventing this particular figure. There is a strong probability that Wodehouse patterned his literary idlers on the models which Munro first drew; Wodehouse, a part-time writer around the turn of the century, must surely have read the *Reginald* stories as they appeared in the *Westminster Gazette.* Wodehouse resigned from the London office of the Hong Kong and Shanghai Bank in 1902 to concentrate on full-time writing, going to work on a London evening newspaper, the *Globe;* thus there is a strong possibility that Wodehouse was influenced by Munro's ideation of the idling, nitwitted *Reginald* type.

Reginald was a success, as far as Munro's work can be termed contemporaneously successful. After it was published in book form in 1904 the volume went to four editions in Munro's lifetime, serving as the cornerstone of his reputation for cynicism, wit, and irreverence. Indeed, if the policeman's lot forces him into daily contact with the depressing, the grimy, the stupid, the ugly, there is no evidence of this experience in the *Reginald* stories, which are so different in tone and subject from a policeman's everyday experiences with crime. *Reginald* may safely be termed the funniest book ever written by an ex-policeman.

CHAPTER 4

The Foreign Correspondent

LIKE his original decision to earn a living by writing, the details of Munro's engagement as a foreign correspondent are hardly touched upon in his sister's biography. She wrote of this second crucial point in his writing career: "In 1902 he was in the Balkans as correspondent for the *Morning Post*." [1] Who interviewed Munro for this job, who catechized his knowledge of the Near East, who passed on his qualifications as a foreign correspondent, and what salary he agreed to are all matters for conjecture. In his writing Munro never gave any information on these points, but it may confidently be assumed that the *Morning Post* paid Munro well; it was a wealthy paper and was not niggardly to its employees.

Munro was certainly dependable and capable enough to represent the paper abroad. He had the indispensable ability to find reliable sources, and he was to display a rather Machiavellian talent for enlisting his own agents and spies to help him in his newsgathering. He was an adept at traveling when that activity was a minor art and not the comfortable pastime it is today. In short, Munro was energetic, enterprising, and imaginative in discharging his correspondent's duties; and his adventurous spirit atoned for any physical debility he may occasionally have suffered. The *Morning Post* acknowledged Munro's daring in its obituary of him:

> His connection with the *Morning Post* began when troubles broke out in Macedonia, in 1902, when he acted as Correspondent for us. Later he became our Special Correspondent in Russia in the troublesome years of 1903–05. He was in St. Petersburg on the fatal Red Sunday of 1905, and was at Warsaw in the days of the Revolution. In all these adventures Mr. Munro displayed an undaunted courage and an enterprise that no discouragement of circumstances could quench.

Again and again he took with a frolic welcome the gravest risks in order to serve the newspaper to which he was accredited.[2]

Although Munro made his start in journalism on the Liberal *Westminster Gazette*, he found that the London *Morning Post* was a more congenial outlet for his product. Founded in 1772, the *Morning Post* had maintained throughout all the successive triumphs and vicissitudes of British history a rigidly Tory stance. It was a newspaper of such Conservative tone that it might more accurately be described as reactionary. The paper invariably bridled at any suggestion of change or improvement in the existing social order, a viewpoint that approximated Munro's, who, although he recognized that it was a poor, shoddy, ignorant world, did not feel that it ought to be altered in any way. Munro believed that this was indeed an ordered universe and that everyone should be, if not happy, at least resigned to his place in it.

The *Morning Post* had become the spokesman for the very best bred people; it was unashamedly snobbish, and it effectively excluded the uneducated from its readership by its attitude of learned superiority. The fact that it had such contributors as Maurice Baring and Hilaire Belloc may serve to mark the intellectual level of the paper's editorial content and the quality of its clientele.[3] As the newspaper of the aristocracy and nobility, the *Morning Post* advertisements were a guide to the Establishment's activities: traveling abroad; going to crammers' schools; patronizing luxurious shops; attending concerts and the theater; and hiring the domestics who abounded in that era—the butlers, maids, valets, coachmen, and footmen. And the court circular and the birth, deaths, and weddings of Establishment types were prominent daily features. The accounts of the activities of Britain's uppermost beings, the country's crust, were interspersed with articles written in a literate, slightly disdainful, and politically safe manner which was pleasing to old school tie wearers.

Going to work for the *Morning Post* was, therefore, a spiritual coming home for Munro.

I *"The Disturbed Balkans"*

Munro went to the Balkans in late 1902, an area which was, in Ethel's words, "a part of the world that had always attracted him."[4] This attraction must have been that of opposites—the ignorant, superstitious, and often illiterate natives of the region being observed and reported on by the urbane and enlightened young man who went to live among them. Munro's affection for these backward lands was apparently genuine; he wrote in his short story "The Cupboard of the Yesterdays" that the Balkans were

> the last surviving shred of happy-hunting ground for the adventurous. . . . When I was a child one of the earliest events of the outside world that forced itself coherently under my notice was a war in the Balkans. . . . It seemed a magical region, with its mountain passes and frozen rivers and grim battlefields, its drifting snows, and prowling wolves; there was a great stretch of water that bore the sinister but engaging name of the Black Sea—nothing that I have ever learned before or after in a geography lesson made the same impression as that strange-named inland sea . . . there is a charm about these countries that you find nowhere else in Europe, the charm of uncertainty and landslide.[5]

Traveling under the auspices of a great British newspaper, Munro first went to Bulgaria, where he was elected a visiting member of the Union Club, a British oasis in wild and woolly Sofia. After a side trip to Vienna in mid-January of 1903 to observe the rowdy conduct of the Austro-Hungarian legislature, the Reichsrath, he returned to Sofia to attend sessions of the Bulgarian legislative body, the Sobranje. He reported on this on January 23, 1903:

> The sittings of the National Sobranje are held in a spacious, square, white-and-gold toned chamber, with lofty galleries on three sides and the fourth dominated by a high balustraded dais, on which beneath a large velvet-draped oil painting of the Prince, stands the lion-blazoned throne-chair. On two descending tiers, upholstered in scarlet, are the seats of the President and the ministers facing the semi-circular dark-wood benches, on which are arranged the elect. . . . In leisurely fashion the members drift into their places, some clad on an irreproachable Westminster model, many in a primitive and uncompromising garb, and one political group affecting a red fez headgear.[6]

Munro was not fluent enough in Bulgarian to follow the debates in the Sobranje, but he wrote to Ethel that "I have voluminous discussions in French with some of the leaders in the Bulgarian Parliament. I don't mean to say the discussions take place there; mercifully neither can criticize the other's accent."[7]

His short story "The Cupboard of the Yesterdays" also touches on his attempts to learn Bulgarian, which being a cognate of the Russian he already knew, could not have been too difficult to apprehend: "I remember a man at Sofia who used to teach me Bulgarian in a rather inefficient manner. . . . After I left Bulgaria he used to send me Sofia newspapers from time to time. . . . And then I heard afterwards that some men came in one day from Heaven knows where, just as things do happen in the Balkans, and murdered him in the open street."[8]

Sofia at that time was colorful enough for the most exotically minded traveler. The town lay on a plateau beneath a ring of snow-capped mountains, and the native Slavs were intermingled with Turks, Vlachs, gypsies, and other flotsam of the Balkans in a gratifyingly picturesque mixture. Men, dressed in sheepskin coats and white trousers, brought their farm produce to noisesome Sofia markets in bullock carts drawn by black buffalo or white oxen. And probably the most bizarre touch of all was the sight of mosque and minaret, the pervasive Balkan influence of Islam. Ethel described her brother's mode of life in the Balkans thus: "To find a horse to ride, a river to bathe in and a game of tennis or bridge, were his first considerations after work had been seen to."[9]

In the spring of 1903 the *Morning Post* sent Munro from Bulgaria to next-door Macedonia to report on the imminent revolution there. The Balkan peninsula at that time was still largely a part of the Turkish Empire, which took in most of the territory between the Black Sea and the Adriatic. There was, of course, no Yugoslavia nor an independent Albania; and Greece extended only briefly above the Peloponnesus. The province of Macedonia was an integral part of Turkey, although its population consisted mostly of fiercely independence-minded Bulgarians, Serbs, and Greeks, who yearned for the day when they should return to their respective motherlands and live under independent Christian rule. Other powers coveted part or all of Macedonia—Bulgaria, Austria-Hungary, and Serbia. The Turkish Empire braced itself for any incursions by these countries in a posture reminiscent of a tiger guarding its kill.

Into this writhing vipers' tangle Munro ventured in April, 1903. He went first to the provincial capital of Macedonia, Üsküb, or Skoplje, as it is now known. He sent back dispatches of the violence and anarchy he found there, so that the readers of the *Morning Post* could absorb the details of the bloodshed with their heavy, silver-laden breakfasts. Reports of still greater trouble came in from Salonica, the big seaport of Macedonia; and on April 30 Munro traveled there in search of more violence with which to titillate his readers. Ethel reprinted the *Morning Post* dispatch which gave Munro's own account of this journey. He was arrested in the Salonica railway yards by Turkish troops and very nearly shot as a suspected dynamiter. Presumably this dispatch is reproduced in Ethel's biography to show the kind of derring-do a newspaper man was expected to perform in the Balkans of 1903.[10]

Salonica was crawling with the saboteurs and guerrillas who had made Turkish rule over Macedonia more repressive and brutal than ever. Munro reported from Salonica on May 3, 1903:

> In company with other correspondents I was taking luncheon in a restaurant opposite the Hotel d'Angleterre, when two reports sent everyone to his feet. On getting into the street I saw a young Bulgar lying in the roadway outside the telegraph office, apparently not quite dead. . . . In another minute several soldiers had run in and extinguished any spark of life that may have been in him. . . . A bomb and two bars of dynamite were found on him. According to the official report . . . he had endeavoured to make his way into the office by representing that he had business to transact. . . . The Bulgar made an attempt to get out his bomb, and he was shot in the struggle which ensued.[11]

Munro moved to Monastir to report other bloody aspects of the revolt, returned to Salonica and Üsküb, and in June, 1903, he rushed into Serbia to report on the assassination of that country's King Alexander and Queen Draga. He wrote from Belgrade on June 13: "I have had a conversation with the gentleman . . . from whom the axe and candles were requisitioned for forcing an entrance to and searching the Palace. . . . The King and Queen were discovered in a small, curtained recess in the Queen's dressing-room. They were killed together, and their bodies thrown out an hour later . . . six hundred officers were implicated in the plot. . . . The only regret expressed in connexion with the whole affair is a formal apology for borrowing the candles at so late an hour." [12]

In the early part of the next year, 1904, Munro reported to the *Morning Post* on Serbia, in dispatches now generically headed "The Disturbed Balkans" and with the byline "From Our Special Correspondent, H. H. Munro." In his dispatches from Belgrade there was not nearly so much violence to report, so that he was able to send back descriptive articles and "think pieces" on local politics. The people of that day, with no television sets or newsreels to inform them about current events, relied upon the correspondents to their newspapers to tell them what was going on in the more primitive parts of the globe. Munro was catering to this need in the dispatch he sent from Belgrade on February 23, 1904:

> The "Big Lent" of the Orthodox Church . . . has entered upon its first week, and for a period of nearly fifty days the rigidly devout will fare little better as to menu than the inhabitants of a besieged and scantily-provisioned city . . . it is probably the unsophisticated peasants of the poorest class who observe the Lenten fast with the greatest scruple, and . . . judging from what one sees as one rides through the arable uplands the task of the husbandman is not lightened by the employment of anything modern and improved. . . . In the cafés and restaurants of Belgrade the billiard tables are decorously swathed in their night-covers, cards and dominoes are banished, and even the placid joys of chess are discountenanced . . . but Belgrade is a place where impressions die young. At such of the restaurants as possess a stage and a company of performers the curtain rises as usual, after the evening meal, on an entertainment of a *café chantant* nature in which the Puritan atmosphere is not conspicuous.[13]

In general, Munro's correspondence from Serbia dealt with Austria-Hungary's designs on Serbian territorial integrity, and with the inevitability of a general war among the Balkan countries. Both of these prognostications were to come true within ten years of Munro's writing them, when the gaggle of nations surrounding Turkey in the Balkans threw her out of Europe, and when Austria-Hungary set the whole world on fire in an attempt to absorb Serbia.

Munro had a facility for puncturing the pretensions of governments about their honor and their ultimate intentions, and he seemed to delight in exposing in the press their apologists. He saw that the ultimate intentions of the governments of all the countries of the Balkans, big and small, were imperial and dishonorable, and that the Balkan countries in their small-scaled way were preparing, like their sponsors, the big powers of Europe, for a general war. Dispassionately, he sent back his comments on this obvious and hideous fact.

II *In Periodically Occupied Poland*

From Serbia, in that spring of 1904, Munro was sent to Warsaw, which was then in a part of Poland occupied by Imperial Russia. When he crossed the Russian border by train from Austria-Hungary, he reported a three-hour delay at the frontier. The Russians had protected their realms against the dangers of Western contamination and invasion by building their railway tracks on a wider gauge than the rest of Europe, so that trains privileged to enter Russia had to be converted to the new rails. Finally arrived in Warsaw, Munro settled into the respectable, stable existence of a tenant in a flat, in this first really big city of his correspondent's experience. He found Warsaw to be more Latinized and Western than the places he had seen in the Balkans, yet there was here the same feeling of living on top of a suppressed nationalism. Warsaw was then more than a hundred miles inside Russia, because Poland at the time was suffering under one of its periodic partitions among its bigger neighbors. The fact that Poland's capital was in Muscovite hands was an ever-present thought in the mind of the average Warsovian.

In his dispatch of March 31, 1904, Munro sent back his first impressions of Warsaw:

> Warsaw has become a veritable human hive of labour and production. For this result it is partly indebted to its favourable geographical situation, which marks it out as a national centre for the commerce of Eastern Europe . . . the Russian system of drastic industrial protection has . . . called into existence a whole growth of home products . . . the security of an assured market has stimulated domestic competition . . . over-production in its turn usually finds a speedy corrective in the growing needs of a growing and thriving population . . . the tramway system is inferior to those of Sofia or Belgrade. As for the horses, they are as wretched and ill-cared for as those usually to be found in Slav countries. . . . The Russians themselves have little direct share in the city's commercial activity; beyond the

garrison, the police, and the majority of higher civil officials, there is not a large Russian element.[14]

One of Munro's most fervid enthusiasms, his passionate interest in the lands and peoples of central Asia, crops up repeatedly in his work and gives it much of the "Saki" cachet of exoticism. In his piece from Warsaw on April 27, 1904, he was able to record, somewhat enviously, some one else's firsthand impressions of this desirable area; and the dispatch gave him the pretext to write about the outlandish places to which he felt so attracted:

I have just had an interview with Mr. James Locke, an American traveller . . . the course of his wanderings led him through Russian Turkestan, across the Oxus into the more or less independent Emirate of Bokhara, and again into Russian territory in the Ferghana district. Sitting in a room which had its floor and furniture strewn with a picturesque litter of Bokharan, Kirghis, and Turkestan costumes, draperies, ornaments and hookahs, the traveller gave me his impressions of the countries he had visited. . . . The railway which connects European Russia with the wild stretch of steppe and mountain chain is well laid. . . . The Turkoman tribes and the wild Aryan horsemen that replace them east of the Oxus, the Usbeks and the Tadshiks. . . . Bokhara, the capital, as Mr. Locke saw it today, is probably the most Oriental city in Asia, with the exception of Lhasa. By day its most salient features are camels, carpets and sweetmeats; by night the European stranger is well advised to leave it to itself.

Munro's vicarious pleasure in setting down the roll call of these place names and nationalities is obvious, but he also had a more serious purpose in mind. He knew that his readers, who had among them a high percentage of British Army officers, would be deeply interested in any eyewitness account of Russian military capabilities. The Russians were thought to be capable of attacking some day the British holdings in south Asia, and in particular in making a strike at India through Afghanistan. This typically Tory fear was apparently shared by Munro himself, for he continued in his dispatch:

The question I pressed was how far the region in general was capable of supplying the wants of an Army. Apparently it would provide a poor foraging ground, except for the items of mutton, remounts and transport animals. . . . But, according to Mr. Locke's personally-formed opinion, Russia's most valuable asset in these regions on the occasion of military emergency would be the goodwill and fighting qualities of the inhabitants. . . . The Russian officers who are on service along this frontier express themselves confident in the event of a Central Asian campaign, of being able to strike an irresistible blow against the enemy.[15]

His dispatch of May 1, 1904 is invaluable for an insight into Munro's deep repugnance when he actually witnessed cruelty. On this Warsaw May Day of 1904 the Russian masters used cruelty, coldbloodedly wielded, to cow the restive Poles. Like most of Warsaw, Munro anticipated great trouble; and to observe it as panoramically as possible he took up a teatime post in a friend's apartment:

In choosing a house on the Ujazdowska Alee for my rendezvous I was guided by the consideration that it was flanked by a large private yard in which Cossacks and police were sure to be quartered.

On arrival, about four o'clock, I found the yard in possession of a half-sotnia of Orenburg Cossacks and about a score of mounted gendarmes, while an outhouse had been improvised into a police office, and a cellar was being prepared as a temporary lock-up. . . . The Cossacks wore the flat Russian service cap instead of the fur shapka of the typical Cossack uniform. . . . It was a composite crowd in which the labouring-class element was not very strongly represented. And except that the throng swelled in numbers and hung inert round certain cross-roads it could not be said to indulge in actual demonstration. . . . Except for the impatient clanging bells of the horse trams a wierd stillness brooded over the allee, while the human mass edged itself blacker and blacker across the roadway. On every balcony could be seen groups of spectators. . . .

And then of a sudden the police on foot made a rush to thrust back the pressing crowds, and a human hurricane of fear and anger voiced in human shrieks broke out on all sides. The mounted gendarmes came out in a scrambling gallop . . . and gorgeously uniformed police officials rushed hither and thither with hoarse screams of "Nazad" (back) and threats of firing. . . . A thin stream of arrested persons began to dribble in . . .

. . . order was given to call out the Cossacks, who were waiting in reserve. . . . The police continued to haul captured individuals into their yard, and I saw a man being subjected to a certain amount of rough treatment on his way thither. I went round to the side win-

dows, which gave me a view of the more private proceedings. . . .
the police, on getting their man into a quiet corner, were not quite aware that their position had been outflanked. One seized the prisoner by the hair and held him, while four others kicked him and beat him with their scabbarded swords and thick sticks. This went on for about two minutes . . . the victim was kicked and beaten until he disappeared into the police office. These men, be it understood, were not Cossacks but Russian police. When the foreign gendarmerie officers have succeeded in establishing European methods of discipline in Macedonia there is a field for their services in Warsaw.

Another man was dragged in half fainting, with his face a mass of blood; he was too dazed to need holding so his captors set on him and kicked him at their leisure . . . three tall policemen marched into the yard with a small newsboy of about ten years old, but the comedy evaporated when they began the same process of beating and kicking him, thrusting him among the dismounted Cossacks so that they might lend a hand . . . he was allowed to escape . . . the child reeled out of the yard, holding his head with both hands. . . .

Out in the allee a policeman was beating two women who would not get out of his way fast enough. . . . Exactly a twelvemonth ago I was at Salonica in the midst of an attempted revolution . . . here in Warsaw the people were not throwing bombs and blowing up public buildings; they were not even throwing stones and smashing windows. . . . The majority, perhaps, had never left the sidewalk. They were simply indulging in a silent demonstration against a Government which certainly does not labour to endear itself with the people. . . .

If these things were done in some Turkish province it would be correct to indulge in rhetoric about "the sands running out." [16]

There are evidences in Munro's dispatches from the Balkans that there was widespread hope in the occupied territories for eventual deliverance from Turkish rule. In his pieces from Poland, however, Munro gives the impression that the Poles had very little hope of ever overthrowing the Russian occupiers, who seemed to have their country by the throat. Yet this discouraging atmosphere helped Munro to profit by his Polish sojurn: the sights and the impressions he absorbed there of the pervasive sense of loss of nationhood and of the hopelessness of attempting to overthrow alien domination were dredged up from his memory eight years later, when he composed his second novel, a shamefaced account of a potential British military disaster, *When William Came*.

III *To the Heart of Darkness*

In the autumn of 1904 the *Morning Post*, anticipating great disturbances and bloodshed, providently sent Munro into St. Petersburg, then the capital of Russia. As he had in Warsaw, Munro rather stodgily took up residence in a flat; and Ethel soon arrived from England to act as her brother's housekeeper. "The evening generally saw us at the telegraph office," Ethel wrote, "where Hector sent off his report and where we met other journalists doing the same thing." [17]

Munro's knowledge of the Russians and of their language, which had heretofore come entirely from books, was now violently amplified by contact with the real thing. The violence with which this introduction took place is reflected in his St. Petersburg correspondence, which frequently reads like a reprise of *The Rise of the Russian Empire*, that conscientously violent book. The Imperial Russian autocracy under Tsar Nicholas II was spread over a variety of countries and peoples from the Pacific to the heart of Europe, an empire whose despotic rule was made unbearable by an Asiatic inefficiency and corruption. The great mass of the population was ignorant and illiterate and had almost no opportunity for betterment or advancement. Democracy in any form would be a most dangerous thing for backward Russia, Nicholas and his supporters believed; and absolutist rule by the aristocracy under an autocrat was the only possible way to govern Russia. But the masses were ripe for a degree of liberalization under a constitution, and the Russian atmosphere was explosive. To Munro, the observer from a happier land which was a sort of democracy, the situation was most interesting, highly newsworthy, but more than a little sad.

He reported on various manifestations of the population's sullenness, stressing the popular resentment of the inefficient handling of the Russo-Japanese War. Sometimes he showed a prescience, a near-clairvoyance in reporting news that foreshadowed great historical events, as when he wrote gracefully and under pressure in his dispatch of Saturday, January 21, 1905, of the imminent general strike of St. Petersburg's laboring class:

Last night a Russian acquaintance came with nervous inquiry as to whether or not I would care to visit the headquarters of the delegates who are directing the workmen's movement, situate somewhere in the outskirts of the city, and a few minutes later we were in a small café on the Nevski swallowing hot coffee to keep out the cold on a long sleigh ride. . . . Getting a sleigh was not an easy matter. . . . A more enterprising izvoshtchik at last undertook the journey, and we were borne out of the light and gaiety of the town's centre into unknown regions, bordered by frozen canals and rime-coated trees. . . .

The voice of the izvoshtchik ran on, keeping time to the thud, thud of the horse's hoofs on the frozen snow, and the landscape underwent rapid changes, growing weird and unreal under the midnight sky. Long lines of empty, harsh-lined factories, fenced round with high wooden structures, rose up now on each side of the deserted roadway and here and there . . . stood quaintly-designed churches, cutting the skyline with an extravagant medley of domed and twisted cupolas, each shooting up a carved and gilded Eastern cross. . . .

Wider and more straggling grew the roadway and its line of wayside houses . . . and then a further change brought back the tall, dreary factories and some idea that we were near our destination. Our first cast was an unlucky one; we drove through a group of astonished gendarmes into the outer yard of the Putiloff works, where a sentry with gleaming bayonet seemed entirely nonplussed by our arrival. A civilian put us on the right track, and we pulled up at last at a short distance from a low wooden building at the door of which a double stream of workmen and youths was entering or issuing. At the same time we were pounced on and interrogated as to our identity and business, and then hurried through the meeting room, where a crowd swarmed around a group of speakers, to a still more crowded inner room, where our reasons for coming underwent further scrutiny. Old men of Garibaldian aspect and young men . . . and toil-smeared workmen who might have stepped from the pages of a Gorki novel . . . looked with undisguised interest at the journalist from a foreign land. . . . Then a door was opened and we were conducted across a yard deep in snow . . . to what was evidently the private headquarters of the movement. A brick oven built round a large chimney took up a greater part of the outer room, beyond which was a sleeping-room where a tired-out organizer lay stretched in deep slumber. . . . On the wooden walls were two or three ikons, with little lamps aglow in front of them. . . . A door led into a further room, long and narrow, lit with one small window and empty of furniture. . . . Kneeling on the floor in the circle of light thrown by a single lamp, a young man was dipping sheets of paper into a black shallow pan which looked like a kitchen utensil. Each sheet was pressed down with a wooden roller, and came out with an impression of the manifesto to the workmen lithographed on its surface. By to-morrow afternoon that proclamation, so humbly turned out, will be in print in the columns of newspapers half the world over. Chairs were brought for us to sit on, while delegates dropped in one by one and gave us the sum and substance of the worker's grievances and demands, which tended in a political rather than an industrial direction.

Through all the men's discourse ran an exultant note as though they were assured that the supreme moment for successful upheaval and social reorganization had at last arrived and that the future was in their hands if they dared to grasp it—and they meant to dare. "On Sunday," they said, "you shall see. The very children are telling each other: On Sunday we will go to the Winter Palace and make the Emperor give us a Constitution. You shall see." By the time this is in print we shall have seen.[18]

And on the next day, Sunday, January 22, 1905, the world indeed saw the Russian people's appeal and their government's brutal answer to it; and Munro was an involved recorder and unshrinking witness to the barbarity of "Bloody Sunday."

A Russian priest, Father Gapon, led delegations of workers, who with their families and adherents numbered two hundred thousand, from the Putiloff Iron Works, from the factories, and from the Neva shipyards to the Winter Palace at the center of the city. These people wanted to present, very humbly, their many grievances to their Little Father, Tsar Nicholas; but, unknown to these swarming petitioners, the whole Imperial family had moved out of St. Petersburg to the safety of a palace at Tsarkoe Selo, in the nearby countryside.

In St. Petersburg, the huge square in front of the Winter Palace was occupied by armed troops. When the hordes of unarmed demonstrators approached the Palace down the radiating boulevards and bridges, cavalry charged them and tried to drive them back; but the protestors moved inexorably in. When the crowds were on the edge of the sacred area in front of the Winter Palace, the troops were ordered to fire into their massed bodies.

Ethel wrote a detailed account of her brother's conduct on this day:

He always lunched at the Hotel de France, which was quite a club for journalists . . . being close to the Nevsky Prospekt, it was the hub of St. Petersburg. . . .

Knowing that there was likely to be trouble, Hector settled that we must go early to the Hotel de France that Sunday, which by its close proximity to the Palace was the best centre from which to watch events. We were joined at the hotel by a Polish friend and lunched quickly.

Hector and the Pole then went out to scout, leaving me in the smoking-room to watch the street and the archway leading to the Winter Palace.

They soon returned at a trot with a lot of others, troops being in possession of the Palace square, allowing no one to enter it. . . .

The crowds were curious to see what was going on in the square, but soon came scampering back, being driven by Cossacks, who were using their whips freely. A second time they tried, and this time the Cossacks charged them with drawn swords. Hector and the Pole had gone out by another exit to the Moika Embankment, and a page presently came to fetch me to them. Here we waited for something to happen. Meanwhile the troops in the Palace square had fired on the deputation arriving by the bridge, and here there was great slaughter.

Thinking nothing would happen on our side of the hotel, I went in, and immediately soldiers arrived on the scene and fired three volleys. Hector and his friend pressed themselves flat against a doorway; a bullet whizzed past Hector's head and lodged a foot off in the wall.

By 2:50 the Palace square was cleared of people and the corpses and wounded were being collected. As Hector had to get all the information he could, he took a sleigh to another part of the city where the fighting was reported to be severe. He got his news, wired to the *Post*, and returned to take me to another hotel, where we dined with one of Reuters' men, who appeared to think the Revolution had begun.[19]

Further observations of Munro's conduct and demeanor during the days immediately following Bloody Sunday are set down in Ethel's biography:

The next two days were very exciting, the Cossacks were doing some killing on their own account. . . . They were an evil-looking lot . . . with criminal faces. Hector scowled so at them as they passed, we being in a sleigh going slowly along rather empty streets, that I hurriedly tried to draw his attention to something on the opposite side of the road, seeing that they were scowling worse at us.

For two nights we had to get back to the flat before dark because the electricians had struck and the lampless streets were not safe. Hector went out to forage and had to run the hardest he knew in one street, an officer shouting that his men would shoot anyone remaining in that street in two minutes' time. . . . He returned with eggs, sweet biscuits, smoked tongue and Bessarabian wine, snatching them up just as the shops, in a panic, were closing. . . .

Hardly had we finished our meal when excited Russians, friends of Hector's, dashed in and gave us the news of the latest Cossack atrocities, pacing up and down the room all the time. It was more exciting than any play. On the second evening, after telling us harrowing tales of searching hospitals for his friend, whom at last he found dead, one Russian calmly invited us to go to the opera with him that night! . . . Hector was making signs at me, behind the man's back, to refuse.[20]

This particular crisis passed, although the Revolution of 1905, whose start is signaled, rampaged on through Russia for months afterward. Munro now had some time to observe the arrogant, conspicuously luxurious existences of the wealthy and fashionable element of St. Petersburg, the privileged and aristocratic stratum that constituted the *ancien régime.* The frost and snow transformed St. Petersburg into a magical setting for this elite who took the air in richly appointed sleds that crowded the snowy quaysides of the frozen Neva, and who thronged the great restaurants, speaking French even more fluently than the headwaiters. The concerts, plays, and ballets of the St. Petersburg season were attended by washed, well-clad, and perfumed audiences; and bemedaled generals at the opera counted the pirouettes of the ballerinas.

Among the capitals of Europe, St. Petersburg was undoubtedly the most corrupt and dissolute; and there is in print a glimpse of Munro observing one aspect of the spectacle: "And in the expensive restaurants, expensive courtesans sat offering themselves for sale where, as 'Saki' said to me, they would not have been allowed to sell white mice." [21] Dispassionately Munro took in all of this glittering putrescence; and, from his observation of the top layer, he drew the Russian Princess and Countess in *Reginald In Russia;* for with his polished manners, his fluent French, his éclat as the representative of England's most snobbish newspaper, he was taken to the bosom of St. Petersburg society.

Violence would still occur occasionally around the city and Munro would report on it with fearless involvement. His dispatch of November 10, 1905, about the Kronstadt mutiny on an island in the St. Petersburg harbor is typical of his enterprise and daring:

I, with other correspondents, shared a tug, ordinary communication being suspended. Coaling necessities delayed our departure until the evening, and we did not arrive in Kronstadt until ten o'clock last night.

From a distance the flare of burning buildings rose above the harbour lights. We found the wharves and quays absolutely deserted. Having scrambled ashore over dredger barges we passed through silent and empty streets. No living soul was visible until we reached the public square . . . the soldiers merely stared at the apparition of three unconcerned pedestrians.

Every house was bolted and barred. . . .

Gathering the details of recent events from other sources with much difficulty we learned that the outbreak originated on Wednesday evening among the sailors in the naval depots. . . .

When I left the town was still wrapped in terror-stricken silence and here and there burning buildings were spreading a flickering glow.[22]

The reporting of continued unrest and frequent violence was Munro's lot for the remainder of his stay in St. Petersburg. The so-called Revolution of 1905 ran its course throughout the following year, and there were outbreaks of arson and bloodshed all over the Russian countryside, a phase of the population's unrest that seemed particularly upsetting to Munro. Here undoubtedly is the source of the jacquerie theme which he used several times in his short stories.

The Emperor Nicholas finally granted a fairly representative parliament, or Duma, to his subjects, and Munro reported on the opening of the Duma on May 10, 1906:

The tiers to the right of the throne began to fill with marshalled groups of Ministers of State, counsellors, Court functionaries, officers of the highest grade of military and naval rank, and the Envoys and Ambassadors of foreign Powers. . . .

Suddenly the peacock assemblage stiffened itself as a long dark stream of roughly-clad humanity poured silently into the assigned space . . . at about half past one . . . the slow approach of the Emperor's procession. . . . The Emperor, the Empress, and the Dowager Empress halted in the centre of the hall. . . . He . . . commenced reading the speech opening his first Parliament. . . . His Majesty's manner was cold and perceptibly nervous. . . .

The Imperial procession re-formed . . . the last member of the Imperial party had left the hall. . . . If autocracy were indeed surrendering, it was marching out with the full honours of war. And the "if" is important.[23]

Maurice Baring supplanted Munro later in 1906 as the *Morning Post*'s correspondent in St. Petersburg, and Munro moved on to Paris to represent the *Post* there. There is something anticlimactic about Munro's assignment to civilized Paris after the nearly four years of violence, bloodshed, and mass murder he had seen in the Balkans, Poland, and Russia. But without difficulty Munro shifted from writing about moody Slavs to ebullient Gauls, successfully making the transition from semi-barbaric St. Petersburg to the epitome of everything urbane and cultured, Paris, the city which in its sleekness and sophistication so closely resembled the paper world of "Saki's" fiction. Ethel noted of his rather surprising writing regimen in Paris: "In addition to writing for the *Morning Post* he wrote some articles in French for a French paper, but not regularly, I think." [24]

From Paris Munro sent dispatches on art shows, balloon races, operas, *haute cuisine*, life along the boulevards and the French character, but mostly he reported on the activities of the Chamber of Deputies, even writing of one of the *opéra bouffe* duels that occurred in the Chamber from time to time: "The duel between M. Benoist and M. Berteaux took place today without either combatant being injured, two pistol shots were exchanged, and the adversaries were forthwith reconciled and able to fill their accustomed places at the afternoon sitting of the Chamber." [25]

IV *A Viewpoint Confirmed*

The years Munro spent in the Balkans and in Russia enabled him to slake his thirst for the exotic. He appreciated this primitive corner of Europe with its backward life and its wild and often ruggedly beautiful landscapes for its rarity in the most cultivated and civilized of continents. The flavor of Graustark and Ruritania so evident in his fiction is authentic enough; he had lived in such an atmosphere. In this regard A. A. Milne has described the rather intimidating impression Munro made upon the other writers of fiction who contributed to the London press fifty-odd years ago: "A strange, exotic creature, this Saki. . . . For we were so domestic, he so terrifyingly cosmopolitan. While we were being funny, as planned, with collar-studs and hot-water bottles, he was being much funnier with werewolves. . . . Our little dialogues were between John and Mary, his, and how much better, between Bertie van Tahn and the Baroness." [26]

The superstitions that abounded in the Balkans twanged responsively to a dark part of Munro's nature, his interest in the supernatural; he had an affinity with the peoples of this region who believed literally in vampires. Like the fey country folk of Devonshire before them, these credulous primitives of eastern Europe suggested the use of a dark corner of literature—eerie, supernatural themes and incidents, things which Munro so originally wove into so much of his writing. Munro himself wrote rather eloquently of his foreign correspondent years in a passage that is a curious blend of personal experience and wish fulfillment:

> Making Vienna his headquarters . . . he had rambled . . . through the lands of the Near and Middle East as leisurely and thoroughly as tamer souls might explore Paris. He had wandered through Hungarian horse-fairs, hunted shy crafty beasts on lonely Balkan hillsides . . . threaded his way through the strange racial mosaic of Salonika . . . learned wisdom from a chance tavern companion, one of the atoms of the busy ant-stream of men and merchandise that moves untiringly round the shores of the Black Sea . . . he always managed to turn up at frequent intervals, at ball and supper and theatre, in the gay Haupstadt of the Habsburgs, haunting his favourite cafes and wine-vaults, skimming through his favourite news sheets, greeting old acquaintances and friends, from ambassadors down to cobblers in the social scale. . . . summed up in a phrase: "a man that wolves had sniffed at." [27]

The quality in Munro's work which the critics have almost unanimously found to be predominant, the strange heartlessness and impassivity toward human suffering which appears to be very much like cruelty, was deepened by these years of the foreign correspondent experience. Before that time Munro's writing had, if not a tone of kindness, a sort of sardonic good humor; but the savagery and bestiality he witnessed in the Balkans and Russia had a direct effect upon him afterward.

There can be no understanding of the causes of Munro's consistently dim view of human nature, of poor bloody humanity, nor of his reputation as a "cruel" writer without a thorough consideration of the corrosive effects of his traumatic years in eastern Europe.

Undeniably there is a streak of cruelty running through Munro's fiction, so that the reader sometimes has the feeling that Munro consciously introduced cruelty as a literary device, a writing mannerism that was intended, like Dickens' Joe the Fat Boy, "ter make yer flesh creep." Because of the prevalence of this sort of thing in his fiction, readers often believed that Munro himself was cruel; but all the evidence of Munro's life and character refutes this idea. Sir John Squire wrote of Munro that "In spite of his jokes about all manner of catastrophes he was a sensitive and humane man to whom cruelty was repugnant." [28] Munro's outrage when he was a witness to cruelty is abundantly evident in his dispatch from Warsaw on May 1, 1904, which is quoted from above.

Munro early in his career (and especially in *The Rise of the Russian Empire*) injected many instances of cruelty into his compositions, instances which seemed perilously close to relish and to savoring pain at second hand. Apparently he soon realized that this particular mannerism, however original it may at first have seemed to him, merely distracted his readers from the points he wanted to make. Munro was enough of a moralist to want his readers to see the things he had to show them; almost everything he wrote, no matter how apparently flippant and nonsensical, had some moralistic "message." The last thing Munro wanted to do was to alienate his readers needlessly; the other things he wanted to say were outrageous enough without introducing gratuitous cruelty. One can see a definite amelioration in this unpleasantness between the writing of *The Rise of the Russian Empire* and the short stories written in the early 1900's.

It seems probable that Munro's frequent use of cruelty—or of what seems to be cruelty—is a facet of his complex makeup, the facet that so admired wild birds and animals. Unblinkingly Munro accepted the ruthless law of nature: kill or be killed, eat or be eaten; and he recognized that the life of field and forest was "red in tooth and claw." When he applied this brutal law to mankind, he found that mankind invariably and cravenly failed to measure up to the lower orders of nature which obeyed it with impassivity and courage. In Munro's fiction the wild creatures are never the victims of his cruelty: it is his humans who are the victims of his savaging. It has been said that Munro always remained emotionally a child, that his faculty for sympathy suffered from arrested development; if this is so, then the emotional retardation and the Swiftian preference for the animal kingdom may help to explain why his fiction so often seems cruel or at the very least heartless.

At any rate, this rather special aspect of his writing was always worked smoothly and relevantly into his fiction, implementing the wit, the invention, and the stylishness which all together comprise the "Saki" manner.

CHAPTER 5

The Imperishable Short Story Writer

IN MAY, 1907, Munro was summoned from his post in Paris to the family home in Devonshire, where his father had become gravely ill. Two days after Munro arrived at his bedside the old gentleman died, and to judge by Ethel's comment Munro was deeply affected by the death: "A very close friendship existed between the two. Hector told me afterwards that writing for the papers had lost much of its incentive since he had lost his most appreciative reader." [1]

Munro returned to France, but in the next year, 1908, he came back to England for good. Leaving his job with the *Morning Post,* he exchanged the assured employment of a foreign correspondent for the uncertain existence of a freelance writer. It would appear that now, in his thirty-eighth year, he had come to a final decision about his career: he would concentrate on gaining a niche in contemporary English literature. Rothay Reynolds said that "Munro returned to London in 1908, where the agreeable life of a man of letters with a brilliant reputation awaited him." [2]

Systematically, committedly, Munro began to establish roots in England. He again took a room in London, at 97 Mortimer Street, to serve as a *pied-à-terre* from which to conduct his extremely active social life and his new foray into literature. Number 97 Mortimer Street, a four-story brick building which survived the German air raids of the early 1940's, is just east of Regent Street, four blocks north of Oxford Circus, and close to the great shops, theaters, and restaurants that figure as backgrounds in so much of Munro's work. It is also close to the Mayfair district with its appendage of the streets around Belgrave Square which was then, more so than now, the center of the great houses of the wealthy, the powerful and the noble: practically all of the inspiration for Munro's fictional creation was close at hand.

In Munro's time the neighborhood of Mortimer Street was

sprinkled with the flats of bachelors among a dominance of milliners, tailors, and furriers, establishments which indicated Mortimer Street's secondary position in the scale of socially acceptable London residences. It was not a particularly grand location, but living in Mortimer Street entitled one to invoke the name of fashionable Cavendish Square in one's address; and the Square could be retained, as Munro noted himself in his story "Cross Currents," as "a courtesy title on the principle that addresses are given to us to conceal our whereabouts." [3]

And, during this time of readjustment, he bought a country cottage to which he could escape on weekends to refresh himself after the week's caging in Town. His modest country place, a house in Woodland Way, Caterham, lay in a suitably bucolic, almost primitive atmosphere on the Surrey Hills, although it was only twenty-three miles from London. Ethel, who was his tenant there, made the cottage into "the most delightful home." [4]

In yet another way he settled into a regular existence by frequenting his club, the Cocoa Tree. He went there principally to play cards, it is true, but he absorbed some of the ritual of club life among clubmen of the type that occasionally figures in his fiction. Like his address in Mortimer Street, the Cocoa Tree Club (now defunct) was not out of the topmost drawer. Although the Cocoa Tree had a long and rather gaudy history going back to the early eighteenth century, one making it especially appealing to the tradition-loving Munro, it did not match in wealth or exclusiveness some of the other clubs along St. James's Street or Pall Mall. The Cocoa Tree's membership was socially acceptable enough, but the rather small establishment functioned above the workaday transactions of the firm of gunsmiths who conducted their business on the ground floor. Still, membership in the Cocoa Tree allowed Munro to amplify his association with Britain's moving and shaking class, and it gave his writings about these people even more authenticity.

Munro had organized his life for the systematic creation of fiction, and in his London room or in his Surrey home he began to write the short stories which were now his principal source of income. Evidently, though, he was not able to command very high prices for his short stories: Rothay Reynolds wrote that "He had to earn his living, but he was content as long as he had money to supply his needs. When a friend once suggested a profitable field for his writings, he dismissed the idea by saying that he was not interested in the public for which it was proposed that he should write." [5]

And, besides contributing to the *Westminster Gazette* and the *Morning Post,* he now began to place some of his stories in a weekly magazine, the *Bystander,* a publication which was one of several glossy-paper London magazines that recorded the activities of Society in that day. Its columns carried news of fashionable weddings, court presentations, yachting, polo playing, and opera- and theatergoing; the magazine's social attitude had strong overtones of rugged conservatism, which made it a compatible home for Munro's fiction.

On the *Bystander* Munro was fortunate in having an editor, Vivian Carter, who was charmingly whimsical. Carter felt, for instance, that the *Bystander* would profit from occasionally being edited from abroad; he took his editorial staff to Continental cities like Amsterdam, Paris, and Berlin, so that special editions of the *Bystander* could be issued from these places.[6] The idea so beguiled Munro that he wrote a short story about Carter's innovation, "The Yarkand Manner," in which he stated that a London newspaper transferred "its offices for three or four weeks from Fleet Street to eastern Turkestan." Carter also wanted to transmute the *Bystander* from a social-whirly house organ of the smart set into a British version of the great satirical organs of the Continent, but the insularity of the *Bystander*'s readers mitigated against its ever achieving the bite and perception of the influential German satirical weeklies *Kladderadatsch* and *Simplicissimus.* Munro, of course, would have welcomed any change along these lines in the *Bystander.*[7]

With his fifth book, *The Chronicles of Clovis,* published in 1911, Munro changed publishers from Methuen, who had brought out *Reginald* and *Reginald in Russia,* to John Lane, under whose imprint all of Munro's future books were published. John Lane, another of the major influences upon Munro, was, like the political cartoonist F. Carruthers Gould, a Devonshire man. As a considerably older man Lane was something of a father figure; he was very well acquainted in the world of English literature and London journalism. Like Gould, Lane was also a staunch Liberal in politics who forgave Munro his devastating attacks made in other quarters upon the incumbent Liberal government. Lane's great achievement had been his publication of the *Yellow Book* magazine in the 1890's; he was lampooned by Max Beerbohm for his enterprise in uncovering much of the unconventional literary talent which distinguished that oddly named magazine which has come to typify the decade of the 1890's in England's literary history.

Although Lane was a dedicated discoverer of writing talent, he was a hardheaded business man who, if he could, gave harsh terms to his authors. He was also very indignant if an author had the temerity to introduce a literary agent into a commercial discussion.[8] Munro, on the other hand, though not at all well-off, was rather lordly about such crass considerations. "He cared nothing for money," wrote Rothay Reynolds of Munro;[9] and sister Ethel said that a "characteristic was his indifference to money."[10] Such unconcern, aristocratic in its disdain, naturally helped Lane in his business dealings with Munro; when Munro came to Lane, it must have seemed to the publisher to be the opportunity to strike a very good bargain indeed.

And yet there was something rewarding in this arrangement for Munro as well: John Lane cared rather deeply about the artistic quality of the books on his list; to have Lane's name as publisher below the titles of one's books was to assure, therefore, careful printing, tasteful makeup, and a respectful critical reception. Since Munro was concerned primarily with the acceptance of his work by the "right" audience, his conversion to John Lane made sense artistically.

Because Lane brought out *The Chronicles of Clovis* in America through his New York branch in February, 1913, Munro made an entry into the huge American literary market. Munro's work failed to take hold in prewar America, though. Apparently there was not yet an American audience large enough to appreciate the suave mockeries and immense sophistication of his stories.

Four books of Munro's short stories were published in his lifetime: *Reginald* (1904); *Reginald in Russia* (1910); *The Chronicles of Clovis* (1911); and *Beasts and Super-Beasts* (1914). Two more books of short stories were published posthumously: *The Toys of Peace* (1919), and *The Square Egg* (1924). Because these six books are the bases of the "Saki" reputation, they must be accorded a weight and an importance that Munro himself would hardly have countenanced in any survey of his work. *Regi-*

nald has been extensively discussed in Chapter 3; and, apart from its flippancy and wit, it has none of the typical Munrovian qualities which give the other five collections their special interest.

I *A Most Original Imagination*

One of Munro's writing distinctions is the manner in which he set out his truly unique fantasies. His straightfaced mendacity, for instance, was a frequent manifestation of this quality. Munro's readers knew, of course, that they were having their "legs pulled," but Munro did it with such appropriateness to his premises that the readers accepted it as slightly unfocused truth. Sir John Squire wrote of Munro's embroidery: "'Saki' was a unique example of the man who tells lies with a grave face. . . . He related a fantastic fable with the most matter-of-fact air. . . . Mendacity and credulity were the spectacles in which he chiefly delighted. . . . In the end the reader of 'Saki' is pleased in proportion to the magnitude of the lie." [11] And Munro himself averred that "one-half of the world believes what the other half invents." [12]

In his story "The Background" Munro told of Henri Deplis, a native of Luxemburg, who spends a legacy in Italy getting tattooed all over his torso with a masterly drawing of "The Fall of Icarus." It was acclaimed, wrote Munro, a masterpiece "by all those who had the privilege of seeing it." So beautiful, in fact, was the man's tattooed torso that Italy refused to let Deplis leave the country because he would be violating "the stringent law which forbids the exportation of Italian works of art." And Munro gravely added: "A diplomatic parley ensued between the Luxemburgian and Italian Governments, and at one time the European situation became overcast with the possibilities of trouble." Meanwhile, the tattooed man had joined the Italian anarchists; and at one of the anarchists' meetings "a fellow-worker, in the heat of debate, broke a phial of corrosive liquid over his back. . . . As soon as he was able to leave the hospital Henri Deplis was put across the frontier as an undesirable alien." [13]

Munro's approbation of a character who lives out a lie is evident in the story of "The Schartz-Metterklume Method." A titled young lady who has missed her train at a remote country station is mistaken for the new governess awaited by a Mrs. Quabarl. This rather parvenu mother of four insists upon bundling the young lady off to the Quabarl mansion, where she is supposed to instruct the Quabarl children in languages and history. The young lady rather grimly accepts the mistaken identity; she informs Mrs. Quabarl that she teaches history by the Schartz-Metterklume method, under which the pupils act out events which actually happened in history, and Mrs. Quabarl agrees to the use of this spurious teaching method on her children. The next morning the young lady makes the four young Quabarls act out the Rape of the Sabine Women, which necessitates, among other curious enterprises, the kidnapping of the lodge keeper's two small daughters. This sample of the "Schartz-Metterklume Method" is enough for Mrs. Quabarl; she discharges the pseudo-governess at once, and the young lady, imperturbable as ever, resumes her interrupted train journey. Munro, who obviously approved her duplicity, makes her the one likable character in the story.

A typical handling of fantasy in a convincing manner is found in the story "The Occasional Garden" in which Munro invented a company called "The Occasional Oasis Supply Association." This company, he wrote, would come to the aid, whenever summoned, of those wealthy people who are embarrassed by their "backyards that are of no practical use for gardening purposes" whenever they give luncheons or dinner parties. The "O.O.S.A." will provide special though temporary gardens for luncheons: "a blaze of lilac . . . one or two cherry trees in blossom, and clumps of heavily flowered rhododendrons . . . in the foreground . . . a blaze of Shirley poppies." If a Bishop is coming to lunch, said Munro, then "you get an old-world pleasaunce, with clipped yew hedges and a sun-dial and hollyhocks . . . borders of sweet william and Canterbury bells, and an old-fashioned beehive or two. . . ."

If, however, it is necessary to deflate a patronizing acquaintance, this company furnishes "E.O.N. service," meaning "envy of the neighborhood." A drab backyard "becomes voluptuous with pomegranate and almond trees, lemon groves, and hedges of flowering cactus, dazzling banks of azaleas, marble-basined fountains . . . where golden carp slithered and wriggled amid the roots of gorgeous-hued irises."[14]

In "The Occasional Garden" Gloria Rapsley uses this exotic garden service to stun and silence the odious braggart Gwenda Pottington. And for a while Gwenda is quite subdued by this vision of horticultural splendor, but four days later, long after the garden has been taken back by the "O.O.S.A.," she bursts uninvited into Gloria's house and discovers that the fantastic garden is no longer there. Gloria calmly states that Suffragettes have broken into the garden and destroyed it while they were demonstrating.

In the story of "Cousin Teresa" Munro conveyed his vast amusement at the workings of London's Edwardian equivalent of Tin Pan Alley. A harebrained dabbler in get-rich-quick schemes strikes gold when he composes the couplet "Cousin Teresa takes out Caesar,/Fido, Jock, and the big borzoi." When the enterprising producers of a revue set this "doggerel" to music and introduce it into their show, the public accords it an hysterical success as Cousin Teresa walks across the stage ". . . followed by four wooden dogs on wheels; Caesar . . . an Irish terrier, Fido a black poodle, Jock a fox-terrier, and the borzoi, of course . . . a borzoi."

Munro added that "Packed houses on successive evenings confirmed the verdict of the first night audience . . . the magic of the famous refrain laid its spell all over the Metropolis. Restaurant proprietors were obliged to provide the members of their orchestras with painted wooden dogs on wheels . . . revellers reeling home at night banged it on doors and hoardings, milkmen clashed their cans to its cadence. . . ." The intellectuals invested the jingle with much significance: preachers discoursed from their pulpits on its real meaning; and society dowagers debated "the problematic Aztec or Nilotic origin of the Teresa *motif*," opining that " 'Cousin Teresa' has a genuine message for one. One can't understand the message all at once, of course." [15] So great was the success of "Cousin Teresa" that its author was rewarded by a grateful nation: he was knighted and named in the annual Honours list for his contribution to English literature.

Munro's name for the leading character in this story is typical of his fantastic invention: Bassett Harrowcluff. Munro's names for his characters—such as Waldo Plubely, Sir Lulworth Quayne, and Loona Bimberton—approached the Dickensian in their combination of aptness and improbability. In inventing these unlikely names Munro may have been motivated by the stringent British libel laws, and quite often his creations bear the names of British towns—Courtenay Youghal, Tony Luton, Murrey Yeovil.

Munro's ability first to ideate his fantasies, then to develop them with all sorts of logical additions and reasonable comments, is another of his literary hallmarks.

II *Jaundiced Observer of the Great World*

Truly knowledgeable about the incidents and the backgrounds he was constantly observing in wealthy town houses and at week-end parties in the country, Munro wrote about these rarefied places and their habitués in a rather unflattering way. His was a sort of love-hate attitude; the milieu was Munro's own, the one into which he had been born, but he wrote about it in a dissociated and alienated way. The following passage in *When William Came* more than anything else he wrote expresses this distaste:

> People of our dominant world at the present moment, herd together as closely packed to the square yard as possible, doing nothing worth doing, and saying nothing worth saying, but doing it and saying it over and over again, listening to the same melodies, watching the same artistes, echoing the same catchwords, ordering the same dishes in the same restaurants, suffering each other's cigarette smoke and perfumes and conversation, feverishly, anxiously making arrangements to meet each other again tomorrow, next week, and the week after next, and repeat the same gregarious experience . . . herded together in a corner of western London.[16]

Perhaps the most amusing treatment of this environment is found in "Tobermory," the short story dealing with a cat which is taught to speak English. Tobermory reveals his astounding faculty at a house party, a background Munro knew intimately. Through the cat's observations Munro comments acidulously on the party's guests—the stupid, the calculating, the greedy, the philandering. The hilarious comments are heightened in wit because they are uttered by the cat. "Tobermory," quite possibly the funniest story Munro ever wrote, combines unique fantasy with deep humor. A closer reading of the story, however, reveals the deprecation and the faint disgust Munro felt for all the characters in it, an example of how Munro could draw an attractive background with repulsive figures in the foreground.

In the story of "The Treasure Ship" Munro deals with an attempt to salvage reputed treasure aboard a galleon which has lain underwater off the Irish coast for three hundred years. The one-man salvager discovers not the galleon but the wreck of a modern motor boat, the *Sub-Rosa,* which had gone down a few years before. In a watertight strongbox in the locker of the motor boat the salvager found a list of prominent people who had committed "indiscretions" of an extortionary nature, together with the evidence of these sins. The salvager confronts the most prominent of the people compromised by the papers he has discovered and starts his blackmailing operations with her, implying that he intends to blackmail the other people on the list and to live in ease thereafter. "The Treasure Ship" is one of Munro's deeper probings of the decadence of Society, an implied revelation of the vicious life led by some of the Best People, although he describes none of these things in detail. "Man delights not me," he seems to be agreeing with Hamlet.

In "The Stampeding of Lady Bastable" Munro contrasts the chicanery of a youth who discovers he is about to be victimized with the stupidity of a self-centered dowager, against a background of Munro's specialty, a country house. Mrs. Sangrail wants to visit "up north, to the MacGregors" and intrigues to have her son Clovis "boarded" at Lady Bastable's house for six days while visiting in Scotland. Lady Bastable, in spite of misgivings about Clovis' wildness, agrees to this boarding arrangement only after Mrs. Sangrail offers to cancel a bridge table debt. Clovis is informed at breakfast of this arrangement, which he feels is really a plot, because he also wants badly to visit the MacGregors "to teach the MacGregor boys, who could well afford the knowledge, how to play poker-patience." When Lady Bastable retires in lonely splendor to the morning room after breakfast, to scan the newspapers for any signs of upheaval which might destroy the existing social order, a theory she dearly subscribes to, Clovis rushes up to a knot of the household's servants, crying "Poor Lady Bastable! In the morning-room! Oh, quick."

The servants, including the gardener with his sickle, run after Clovis into the morning room. At the door, Clovis yells to Lady Bastable "The jacquerie! They're on us!" Lady Bastable, after one horrified glance at the onrushing servants, flees out through a French window to the lawn. After Lady Bastable realizes the enormity of this practical joke, she frigidly refuses to board Clovis and pointedly settles the bridge debt. Clovis accompanies his mother to the MacGregors after all.

In a good many of his other stories, in the majority perhaps, Munro took as models the people of this upper world; but he never wrote of them with kindness or approbation. He criticized their habits, their beliefs, their characters; but he never once criticized the social system that permitted such beings to rest on the top of it. Because Munro believed in the rightness and inevitability of the class system, he was incapable of making any fundamental criticism of it. As H. W. Nevinson has stated of Munro, "His nature ranged him on the side of authority and tradition." [17]

These "socialite" stories are the undistorted reflections of his feelings about the people in his own narrow little stratum of humanity. His disenchantment with his peculiarly personal milieu, the fashionable world, is expressed in a manner that transcends in its skepticism, cynicism, and bitter humor the writings of contemporaneous Society wits like Oscar Wilde, W. S. Gilbert, Max Beerbohm, and John Oliver Hobbes. It is not quite accurate, however, to group Munro with such modern writers; his mordancy, from an older tradition, is more akin to the outlook and humor of the Restoration playwrights, to Dryden, Wycherley, and Congreve. Munro felt much the same repelled fascination at the spectacles and excesses of his own Vanity Fair. He took much the same delight, too, in ripping aside the veil of hypocrisy in which the *beau monde* swathed itself. Munro observed the frivolities of the great world with incredulity often, with wry amusement always; his contempt for the pursuits, attitudes, and morals of this upper world invariably leaks through the glossy surface of his stories. Yet the anomaly is that Munro personally was a devout practitioner of all that was conventional and "done."

This way of life was after all his own, and his obedience to its outward aspects went far back into his heritage. And for all Munro's comparative impecuniousness, no one could write more authoritatively than he of a world of stately homes, tailored clothes and handmade frocks, heavy-laden breakfast sideboards, glittering automobiles, elaborate balls and dinner parties, and hovering butlers, footmen, and maids. Munro's writing is archtypical of that halcyon prewar era of Edward VII and George V when, for the consumption of the wealthy and privileged, a caste of loving artisans labored in a small area of London's West End—the tailors, gunsmiths, bootmakers, vintners, hatters, tobacconists, jewelers, and haberdashers whose products play so large a part in Munro's fiction. No other writer has so fully bequeathed the feel and look of this vanished time of apparent solidity and order, when the happy few in Britain led their carefree lives in the country houses of "county" Society or in mansions in the sooty air of Town.

It certainly was not Munro's intention to be remembered solely as the recorder of these Golden Calf years, when the wealthy dissipated and lorded it over a world whose stability and imperviousness to social change seemed eternal. It is amusing that posterity has assigned Munro just this role of recorder of the revels, while it ignores his efforts to write seriously and even profoundly. There is an irony here that would fit well into one of his improbable plots.

III *Contempt for Routine Living*

Another of the themes running through Munro's stories is his disdain of domesticity and a settled, ordered way of life. In "The Mappined Life" Munro deplored the caging of birds and beasts in the London Zoological Gardens, even though the creatures had just been given new and more natural quarters in the Garden's Mappin Terraces, and from this condition he drew a parallel with the self-imposed captivity of the middle-class Londoner. Into the mouth of a young lady who has just visited these new zoological quarters, Munro puts his estimate of her and her kind: "We are just so many animals stuck down on a Mappin terrace, with this difference in our disfavour, that the animals are there to be looked at, while nobody wants to look at us . . . there are heaps of ways of leading a real existence. . . . It's the dreadful little everyday acts of pretended importance that give the Mappin stamp to our life." [18]

In the story "Tea" Munro wrote in more detail of this domestic disaffection: "Cushat-Prinkley detested the whole system of afternoon tea. . . . Thousands of women, at this solemn hour, were sitting behind dainty porcelain and silver fittings, with their voices tinkling pleasantly in a cascade of solicitous little questions. . . . 'Is it one lump? I forget. You do take milk don't you? Would you like some more hot water if it's too strong?' "

Munro made his character, James Cushat-Prinkley, fall in love with a girl because she makes a minimum of fuss when she serves tea: "Cushat-Prinkley found that he was enjoying an excellent tea without having to answer as many questions about it as a Minister for Agriculture might be called on to reply to during an outbreak of cattle plague." After Cushat-Prinkley marries this paragon, however, she reverts to type, serving her first tea as a married woman with a full panoply of porcelain and silver, and asking solicitously: "You like it weaker that that, don't you? Shall I put some more hot water to it? No?" [19]

Munro's approval of a break with the ordered life, a reversal of stodgy living habits into a precarious but exhilarating existence, shines through in his story "The Way to the Dairy." A rather elderly single lady, who had spent a restricted life in very modest circumstances, is left a large inheritance from a distant relative who mentioned no one else in the family in his will. The elderly lady, upon receiving this fortune, is immediately cosseted by three of her nieces, the Brimley Bomefields, who had ignored her when she was poor: they expect now that she will leave her newfound money to them when she dies. Unfortunately, the Brimley Bomefields take her to France; there the nieces give the old lady a hortatory introduction to gaming tables and the life of casinos.

Instead of alarming the old lady, these gambling hells charm her, and she becomes a confirmed gambler. Moreover, she surrounds herself with other gamblers: "For the first time in her life the old thing was thoroughly enjoying herself; she was losing money, but she had plenty of fun and excitement in the process . . . her nieces . . . still remained in attendance on her, with the pathetic unwillingness of a crew to leave a foundering treasure ship which might yet be steered into port." [20] At last, the aunt's continual gambling and her growing circle of raffish friends from the casinos drive the Brimley Bomefields back to England, leaving the old lady to enjoy her newfound way of life. This approbation of dangerous living was not, of course, the majority view; but it is firmly embedded in the "Saki" canon, and one must consider Munro's disgust of domesticity as essential to an understanding of his attitude and work.

IV *A Passion for Wild Things*

Another factor to be considered in assessing Munro is the frequency with which he introduced wild animals and birds with such knowledgeability into his short stories. E. V. Knox has cogently described this aspect of Munro:

> "What an enormous number of animals!" might be the comment of a reader who looks casually through these pages. . . . There is in fact

a Munro menagerie. It is not merely the god Pan nor his rout of sylvans who break into country houses and obstruct the purposes of men. The wild things run riot. They peep out in every plot. They peer from the corner of every conversation. . . . One creature or another, exotic or domesticated, is always playing a part in these tales, and sometimes a decisive part, terrible or whimsical, a *bestia ex machina*. Here is a world in which time after time in the author's eyes, human beings are a little lower than the animals.[21]

And it is true that Munro contrasted the behavior of animals with the behavior of humans, always to the latter's discredit.

In his book *Beasts and Super-Beasts,* which mockingly echoes Shaw's title *Man and Super-Man,* he makes this passion for animals a recurring theme. In this book the short story "On Approval" makes animals the subjects of a series of paintings by a German immigrant artist in London:

His pictures always represented some well-known street or public place in London, fallen into decay and denuded of its human population, in the place of which there roamed a wild fauna, which, from its wealth of exotic species, must have originally escaped from Zoological Gardens and travelling beast shows. "Giraffes drinking at the fountain pools, Trafalgar Square," was one of the most notable and characteristic of his studies, while even more sensational was the gruesome picture of "Vultures attacking dying camel in Upper Berkeley Street." . . . The large canvas on which he had been engaged for some months. . . . "Hyenas asleep in Euston Station" . . . the picture that he showed us last week, "Sand-grouse roosting on the Albert Memorial" . . . a more ambitious picture, "Wolves and wapiti fighting on the steps of the Athenaeum Club." [22]

Perhaps the secret of Munro's love for animals is that, while he recognized their ruthless struggle for survival, he habitually contrasted their instinctive decency and bravery with the sorry spectacle of human behavior. A long expression of this sentiment is to be found in the story of "The Achievement of the Cat":

Confront a child, a puppy, and a kitten with a sudden danger; the child will turn instinctively for assistance, the puppy will grovel in abject submission to the impending visitation, the kitten will brace its tiny body for a frantic resistance. . . . The cat of the slums and alleys, starved, outcast, harried, still keeps amid the prowlings of its adversity the bold, free panther-tread with which it paced of yore the temple courts of Thebes, still displays the self-reliant watchfulness which man has never taught it to lay aside . . . it dies fighting to the last, quivering with the choking rage of mastered resistance.[23]

One would think that, if Munro were ever offered a chance at reincarnation, he would return as some animal. He never lost his fascination with other orders of creatures, even amid the horrors of the battlefield; in his piece "Birds on the Western Front," which appeared in the *Westminster Gazette* a few weeks before his death, he gratefully described the brave behavior of the birds in adversity; and he was ashamed that man's brutality had so gravely damaged their environment. Munro's feeling for birds and animals should not be dismissed as the usual Englishman's love of horses and dogs; it was a much deeper emotion than that. It may be explained as being a reaction to his misanthropy—he had a deep need to admire life, even if it was not that of his own species.

V *Mastery of the Surprise Ending*

The editors of the early 1900's seem to have admired and often to have demanded short stories with surprise endings—a mechanism most notably used in that era by the American short story writer O. Henry (William Sydney Porter). Munro, however, used this device with even greater cleverness and aptness, which was to be expected from the more accomplished of the two writers. Munro and O. Henry both had seen the seamy side of life, the discreditable facets of human nature; but Munro, better educated, more widely traveled, and with a much more sophisticated mind, set his satiric sights higher and was more successful in annihilating his targets. Munro was the more polished stylist, the more original moralist, the more ambitious satirist; and he never stooped to the use of O. Henry's sometimes cloying sentimentality.

Munro may have deprecated this snapper-ending trick as being too facile, but it placated editors who demanded that Munro always write as that startling fellow "Saki." It is difficult to give examples of this aspect of Munro's writing without relating the entire plot of the story in point, so tightly knit was the preparation and skilled placing of false scents; the surprise ending of the story must be considered in relation to every little thing that has occurred before it. O. Henry, on the other hand, often sacrificed credibility in his characters or the careful development of his staging to achieve his trick endings.

In the story "The Bag" a wealthy Russian youth, Vladimir, is visiting an English "county" family that is very keen on fox hunting. Vladimir doesn't ride well enough to join the local hunt, but he does some shooting in nearby woods and fields. When he returns from one of his expeditions, he proudly announces that he has shot an animal that "lives in the woods and eats rabbits and chickens." The family is thunderstruck: "Merciful Heaven! he's shot a fox!" And to do so is just about the worst social blunder one can make in these parts. They order Vladimir to hide his unopened game bag since they are expecting the master of the local hunt to arrive at any minute. Munro skillfully developed the suspense of the inevitable discovery of Vladimir's heinous offense. The hunt master eventually deduces that a fox has been shot by the Russian, and he storms out of the house. Vladimir is then curtly ordered by the household to bury his kill. Munro ended the story: "And thus it came to pass that in the dusk of a November evening, the Russian boy, murmuring a few of the prayers of his church for luck, gave hasty but decent burial to a large polecat." [24]

Another surprise ending capable of being summarized briefly is the ending of "The Forbidden Buzzards." A friend of Clovis Sangrail dearly wishes to propose marriage to Betty Coulterneb, but the girl is attracted to still another man, one Lanner. Clovis' friend appeals to him for help in this situation. When Lanner is invited to the girl's country home for a weekend, Clovis is also there; and he tells the hostess, Betty's mother, that Lanner is really visiting in order to steal the eggs from the nest of two "rough-legged buzzards . . . the only pair of rough-legged buzzards known to breed in this country." These birds have honored the Coulterneb home by nesting in the woods adjacent to it. The hostess is shocked and outraged by Clovis' story, but he suggests that Mr. Lanner never be left alone long enough to perpetrate the egg theft. The hostess agrees to this suggestion, and Mr. Lanner is constantly, if involuntarily, in the company of the governess or the nine-year-old son, or he is being shown all the boring aspects of the house and grounds, or being dragged off to visit a nearby village or some allegedly historic farmhouse. Lanner never has the opportunity to propose to the girl, and Clovis' plot must be accounted successful. Munro ends his narrative thus: "The buzzards successfully reared two young ones, who were shot by a local hairdresser." [25]

Munro's expertise with the surprise ending is testified to by the frequency with which some of his stories employing this device have been reprinted and anthologized: "The Open Window," "Dusk," and "The Reticence of Lady Anne." This surprise ending was a literary trick, no doubt; but it took an able writer to make it credible. Present-day stories which eschew all hints of a plot and attempt to emerge as "mood pieces" or "slices of life" seem somehow skimped and underdone when they are compared with the tailor-made short story of 1910.

VI *Use of the Uncanny*

Munro was the only writer of his day who consistently used the unhackneyed subject of the uncanny and supernatural. Other writers were indifferent to this subject, perhaps because they lacked an inborn feeling for it and in any case could not fit it into their work. And by its nature the subject disqualified itself from use by the realists and social reformers, and probably could only be appreciated by a restricted and selective readership like Munro's. This subject might easily have degenerated into the merely silly, but Munro handled it with gravity and great writing skill, and he was helped in its development by something sympathetic in his nature.

In the story "The Music on the Hill" the sense of foreboding, of being watched by something supernatural, is credibly conveyed. A girl named Sylvia has inveigled wealthy Mortimer Seltoun into marriage; but, because she feels that he is too distracted by life in London, she wrenches him away to his country place, "a remote, wood-girt manor farm." Sylvia, a town-bred girl, does not appreciate this rural setting: " 'it is very wild,' she said to Mortimer, 'one could almost think that in such a place the worship of Pan had never quite died out.' "

Mortimer assures her that the worship of Pan has never disappeared thereabouts. Then, on an excursion into the woods, Sylvia stumbles upon

> a stone pedestal surmounted by a small bronze figure of a youthful Pan . . . a newly cut bunch of grapes had been placed as an offering

at its feet. Grapes were none too plentiful at the manor house, and Sylvia snatched the bunch angrily from the pedestal. Contemptuous annoyance dominated her thoughts as she strolled slowly homeward . . . across a thick tangle of undergrowth a boy's face was scowling at her, brown and beautiful, with unutterably evil eyes. . . . "I saw a youth in the wood today . . . a gypsy lad, I suppose." . . . she went on to recount her finding of the votive offering. . . . "Did you meddle with it in any way?" asked Mortimer . . . "I've heard it said that the Wood Gods are rather horrible to those that molest them. . . . I should avoid the woods and orchards if I were you, and give a wide berth to the beasts on the farm."

The next afternoon Sylvia rambles off, taking care to avoid the farmyard cattle and goats, and staying away from the woods. She climbed through open slopes of heather above the manor, "but across the wooded combes at her feet . . . Sylvia could presently see a dark body, breasting hill after hill . . . at last he broke through the outermost line of oak scrub and fern . . . a fat September stag carrying a well-furnished head." The stag was being pursued by a pack of hounds; but, instead of heading toward safety, he bounded up the hill where she stood:

> Pipe music suddenly shrilled around her . . . and at the same moment the great beast slewed round and bore directly down upon her. In an instant her pity for the hunted animal changed to wild terror at her own danger. . . . The huge antler spikes were within a few yards of her. . . . And then with a quick throb of joy she saw that she was not alone; a human figure stood a few paces aside. . . . "Drive it off!" she shrieked. But the figure made no answering movement. The antlers drove straight at her, but her eyes were filled with the horror of something else she saw other than her oncoming death. And in her ears rang the echo of a boy's laughter, golden and equivocal.[26]

The central figure of the story "Gabriel-Ernest" is a creature who takes the form of a youthful human in daylight but changes into a wolf at night. This werewolf preys upon the wild and domesticated animals of the neighborhood and upon "children when I can get any; they're usually too well locked in at night."[27] In "The Soul of Laploshka," a miser dies suddenly; but, in a circumstantial and logical narrative, his ghost returns repeatedly to disturb his former tormentor.

The supernatural is used both as an actual occurrence and as an example of human credulity in "The Hedgehog." A country house, Exwood, is rented by the Norbury family from a Mrs. Hatch-Mallard. The Norburys are very fond of the house, so whenever necessary they try to please their landlady in the hope that she will renew the lease. The house is supposed to be haunted by a number of ghosts; when a highly clairvoyant woman, the seventh daughter of a seventh daughter, comes to it as a guest, some of the prominent people in the neighborhood wrangle about which ghost she will see. The landlady tells her tenant: "Mrs. Norbury, I shall take it as a deliberate affront if your clairvoyante friend sees any other ghost except that of my uncle." [28]

The Norburys are apprehensive that their clairvoyant guest may see some other ghost; and sure enough, on the third night at Exwood she sees not the ghost of Mrs. Hatch-Mallard's uncle, but a white hedgehog with evil yellow eyes: it crawls across her bedroom, its loathsome claws clicking along the floor, its hideous eyes always staring at her. When it reaches a window, it climbs up on the sill and vanishes. A local history book of the county identifies the hedgehog as the ghost of Nicholas Herison, who was hanged at Blatchford in 1763 for the murder of a farm lad. The tenants, the Norburys, are more than a little perturbed because they remember Mrs. Hatch-Mallard's promise of wrath if her uncle's ghost is not seen. Mr. Norbury thereupon tells a lie to the clairvoyant: the whole incident was only a practical joke; what she saw was really a stuffed albino hedgehog, which he had drawn on a string across the room and out the window, a prank often played on guests. Munro ended the story by noting that Mrs. Hatch-Mallard renewed the lease, but the clairvoyant never renewed her friendship with the Norburys.

Many other incidents and characters from the supernatural can be found in Munro; he dealt with the subject frequently and unexpectedly but in a way pertinent to his stories. The influences of his sojourn in the haunted Devon countryside and in half-pagan eastern Europe have already been marked. His heritage of Celtic blood from generations from the misty Highlands also explains to some extent his wild fancies and his liking for the eerie and macabre. In a true "original," this interest was perhaps the strangest of his writing peculiarities.

VII *Some Other Themes*

Some of Munro's short stories do not fit into any general classification; there is, for instance, the story of "The Sheep." Munro appears to have been a perceptive and quick-witted man, with a high degree of intolerance for people who were born with the opposite qualities of dullness and stupidity; and this story proves that he did not suffer fools gladly. In it Munro allowed his distaste for fools to turn into naked hatred.

The "sheep" of the story is a bungling, clumsy, stupid young man, whose unthinking folly is made all the more irritating by his ineffable self-satisfaction. He is described as ruining a partner's bridge hand, shooting a protected game bird, and losing a local election for a candidate by making a blundering remark at a political meeting. To compound his obnoxiousness, he has become engaged to a desirable and otherwise intelligent girl whose brother despises the "sheep." The terrible ending of the story—not the penultimate description of the fool's death beneath the ice of a skating pond—but the lovingly written details of how a dog which prevented the fool's rescue is thereafter cosseted and coddled by the girl's brother is absolutely counter to all Christian morality, although it is essential Munroism. The virulence of the writing in "The Sheep" which transcends this bitter quality found in so many other of his stories makes the reader doubt Munro's mental balance.

A story which shows that Munro never forgot his circumscribed childhood is "Sredni Vashtar." The central figure of this story, a ten-year-old orphaned boy Conradin is looked after in a house in the country by his middle-aged cousin and guardian Mrs. De Ropp. Mrs. De Ropp is an inept guardian who thwarts Conradin continually "for his own good." Conradin hates her bitterly, although he is able to dissemble his hatred. The only place on the property where he is his own master is an unused tool shed in a hidden corner of the garden; here he keeps a rather bedraggled hen, which he dotes on, and in a dark corner, securely caged, a large ferret "which a friendly butcher boy had once smuggled, cage and all, into its present quarters, in exchange for a long-secreted hoard of small silver."

Conradin, although terrified of the sharp-fanged ferret, adores it, and begins to worship it as a god. Conradin, who names it

"Sredni Vashtar," regularly brings it offerings of red flowers and scarlet berries. After a while Mrs. De Ropp notices Conradin's frequent trips to the tool shed. "It is not good for him to be pattering down there in all weathers" she says to herself; and, visiting the shed, she discovers the hen but not the ferret. When she sells the hen and it is taken away, Conradin's hatred becomes cold and murderous: "In the shed that evening . . . he asked a boon. 'Do one thing for me, Sredni Vashtar.' The thing was not specified. As Sredni Vashtar was a god he must be supposed to know."

Mrs. De Ropp notices that Conradin's visits to the tool shed have not ceased with the removal of the hen. "What are you keeping in that locked hutch?" she demands of Conradin; and, ransacking his bedroom, she finally finds the key to the cage. She marches into the tool shed but she does not come back out:

> Conradin stood and waited and watched. Hope had crept by inches into his heart, and now a look of triumph began to blaze in his eyes. . . . And presently, his eyes were rewarded: out through the doorway came a long, low, yellow-and-brown beast, with eyes a-blinking at the waning daylight, and dark wet stains around the fur of jaws and throat. Conradin dropped on his knees. The great polecat-ferret made its way down to a small brook at the foot of the garden, drank for a moment, then crossed a little plank bridge and was lost to sight in the bushes.[29]

After a long wait Conradin hears the screaming of a maid and a great commotion among the other servants. And, while they argued about who should break the bad news to the poor child, Conradin made himself another piece of toast. "Sredni Vashtar" is one of the most frequently reprinted of Munro's stories; because of its balefulness and horror, it stays in a reader's memory ever afterward. Very clearly, it is Munro's sublimation of his own hatred for his aunt Augusta when he was her unruly ward at Broadgate.

Another of Munro's traits is the effortless display of his cosmopolitanism. In "The Interlopers" he used the background of a forest in the Carpathians for two *mitteleuropa* characters most credibly drawn in this sketch of the old Austro-Hungarian Empire. The story "The Name-Day" also deals with the old Habsburg dominions; and, like "The Interlopers," it conveys the flavor of an exotic corner of the world. "The Wolves of Cernogratz" knowledgeably deals with the fulfillment of a legend in an east German castle, and in "Wratislaw" the badinage between a Gräfin and a Countess somehow imparts the gaiety of old Vienna. Munro casually injected Dieppe, Homburg, the Engadine, Novibazar, Paris, Pomerania, Burma, and other foreign places into his stories, always with the authenticity of having been to these places himself. Just as casually he introduced characters from the Russian nobility, the revolutionaries of the Balkans, the smug merchant class of the Far East, or the bohemian world of Paris; like the exotic backgrounds, these characters were authentic. Munro had known such people.

VIII *Posterity's Verdict*

Although Munro may have written his short stories to satisfy an exigent financial need, making them acceptable to editors rather than trying to make them into little gems of literary art, it is for these short stories that he is remembered today. Posterity, in its dogmatic way, has decided that Munro is to be considered solely as the creator of little, wryly humorous stories. This latter-day judgment can be seen in the extent to which Munro's short stories have been anthologized in collections of humorous stories. A few of Munro's stories, in surveys of modern English literature, have even been held up as worthy examples for the novice writer to imitate; Munro would surely have been amused at such canonization.

But the fact remains that through his short stories alone, and not his other literary achievements, the "Saki" name lives on today; this is borne out by an event of recent days when Munro's stories were given the ultimate accolade of this age—conversion to television material. Thirty-six of Munro's short stories, in eight one-hour programs, were "adapted" for British television audiences. They were later exported to the United States, where they were rather a success with viewers of "educational" stations. Yet, like wine that does not travel well, Munro's bouquet did not come through in this television transmogrification. Of necessity only Munro's dialogue could be used in these television adaptations. The dialogue which was used is amusing enough, but these playlets could not possibly introduce Munro's observations, asides, and comments; these are just the things that complement the dialogue in the short stories to give them the unique "Saki" cachet. At any rate, these television adaptations proved that Munro has some appeal for the latest generation, who would rather get their entertainment from television than from books.[30]

There is a strong likelihood that Munro used some sort of system to help him turn out his short stories in a no-nonsense, workmanlike fashion. Despite his superficial languor—the affectation of the gentleman of that period—Munro was an organized, industrious writer who practiced his calling with seriousness. It is logical to assume that he kept a notebook of plots for possible use in the composition of his short stories, and that his friends and relatives told him anecdotes they thought would be helpful to him. An indication of this practice is in a passage written by the humorist Thomas Anstey Guthrie ("F. Anstey") in March, 1912: "I met Hector Munro (Saki) . . . and he had a soft and remarkably pleasant voice. I find a note of an anecdote he told me that afternoon of a man who when seized by a sudden and violent hunger found that he had nothing but a penny in his pocket. Fortunately, however, he came upon an automatic chocolate machine outside a shop, eagerly put in his penny and got a box of matches." [31]

In Munro's time, editors wanted no part of stories which experimented with plotless plots, stream-of-consciousness monologues, precious obscurity, or any other literary innovation. They were looking for the well-made story which did not flaunt any of the writing conventions, and Munro did not attempt to divert them from this insistence on the well-made story. Almost certainly Munro himself subscribed to this rationale, for Sir John Squire firmly believed in Munro's devotion to traditional writing: "He polished his sentences with a spinsterish passion for neatness and chose his words as the last of the dandies might choose his ties. Writing brief stories and sketches for evening newspapers he was as careful with the shaping of his paragraphs as the most anchorite of esthetes writing for an elect few with glass-fronted bookcases. He expended the pains of a poet upon modern fairy-tales." [32]

On the other hand, A. A. Milne gave his opinion of Munro's craftsmanship in this pronouncement: "I do not think that he has that 'mastery of the *conte*' . . . which some have claimed for him. Such mastery infers a passion for neatness which was not in the boyish Saki's equipment. He leaves loose ends everywhere." [33] But, as Munro himself observed, "Two of a trade never agree." [34]

The "Saki" short stories seem certain to endure; the latter-day reader finds something familiar and pertinent in Munro's cynicism and unflattering view of humanity. Munro's people are alive and contemporaneous: one still sees today the stuffed shirt, the persistent sponger, the social climber, the ambitious young politician, the black sheep, the self-satisfied incompetent, the wealthy idler, the silly, exploited woman, and, even occasionally, the wit. Munro's attractiveness for the modern reader is his surprising modernity.

CHAPTER 6

The Novelist as Purposeful Artist

ALTHOUGH the short stories which Munro produced with such regularity and distinction brought him a fairly good living and considerable éclat, he apparently began to realize that he could not be considered a whole man of letters until he had written a novel. His swarms of short stories, although they were intelligently conceived and impeccably turned out, now had to be implemented by something larger in scope, more ambitious in theme, but of equal distinction in presentation. To judge by its internal evidences, Munro wrote his first novel during the two or three years following his return to London in 1908. This book, *The Unbearable Bassington,* was published in October, 1912.

I *A Rigorously Original First Novel*

For the theme of his book Munro chose the sins of a young ne'er-do-well of the upper middle class, who—by rejecting opportunities of birth, position, and influence—alienated the people who tried to help him while he brought misery to those who loved him, as he obstinately traveled down his own road to perdition.[1] According to Ethel, Munro used a real-life model for his portrait of the *Unbearable Bassington*: "The chief character is taken from life, but the original, so far, has not had a tragic ending." [2] The young protagonist of the book, Comus Bassington, is shown to be a feckless, totally undisciplined, improvident but handsome and charming youth of twenty. Comus frequented the glittering world of London society without having sufficient money to pay for the costly indulgences of that world. His mother, Francesca Bassington, a still attractive widow of forty, could not begin to pay for Comus' extravagances; on the contrary, she wanted Comus to bring security to her by making a wealthy marriage.

Francesca, Munro wrote, "if pressed in an unguarded moment to describe her soul would probably have described her drawing-room."[3] She cherished her furniture, rugs, and knickknacks, in particular a large painting of a battle scene attributed to Van der Meulen. She lived in a mansion in Mayfair that had been bequeathed to her by an old friend, Sophie Chetrof; but Francesca could only occupy—not possess—this fine house until Sophie's niece, Emmeline Chetrof, was married. A few years before the time of the novel's opening Francesca had intrigued to get Comus, then still a schoolboy, to capture Emmeline and eventually marry her—a coup which would insure the continuity of Francesca's residence in the beloved house in Mayfair. And Emmerline, in actual fact, was quite taken with Comus; he could have married her eventually without undue difficulty. But Comus destroyed Emmeline's receptive affection for him by a seemingly deliberate act of cruelty to her little brother, who was at school with Comus. And so the first of Francesca's schemes for Comus was discarded.

Comus was given a second chance to make a profitable marriage when he inaugurated a warm friendship with the young and attractive heiress Elaine de Frey, and a mutual physical attraction developed into a budding love affair. Comus' mother, who took careful note of this affair, was most pleased; if Comus would not or could not earn his own way in the world and live on a sensible scale, then his marriage to an indulgent heiress who would underwrite his bills and preserve his mother's household treasures and comfortable life seemed to be the perfect solution.

But Comus, in his usual self-destructive fashion, threw away once more the opportunity: he committed a series of selfish, blundering misdeeds which alienated Elaine. Comus' mother was deeply disturbed at the son's losing Elaine's hand by his own folly; but, when Elaine married (on the rebound, it is implied) the rising young politician Courtenay Youghal, the mother was doubly annoyed. Comus had come under the influence of Courtenay Youghal, who led a showy and extravagant life. After Francesca had gone to considerable trouble to find Comus a position in the government of an island in the British West Indies, Youghal had been instrumental in abetting Comus to evade taking the job.

In one of several long scenes which are completely irrelevant to the theme of the novel, Courtenay Youghal broke off his relationship with his number one inamorata, whom he quite frankly told he was abandoning in order to marry a wealthy woman who would be able to advance his political career. Youghal admitted to his former girl friend that he felt no deep love but only a kind of affection for the heiress he was going to marry. Since the former girl friend herself was dallying with several other men, she was not unduly troublesome about Youghal's jettisoning of her.

In still another chapter that has no bearing on the main theme of the book, Elaine de Frey, out for a horseback ride in the English countryside, stumbled upon the farm owned by Tom Keriway, whom she had known previously as a wide-ranging traveler who spent most of his time in the wilds of the Middle East. Keriway, who had been forced to return to England because he had lost his health and his money, now led a tame, constricted life. This chapter is apparently a literary sublimation of Munro's own return to England in 1908. Perhaps, as has been suggested in J. W. Lambert's Introduction, he gave up the rootless but congenial existence of a foreign correspondent to return to England to look after his difficult sister. In any event, Keriway's experiences abroad reflect Munro's own aspirations.

In the chapter in which Elaine de Frey informed a cousin and an aunt of hers of her engagement to Courtenay Youghal, Munro vividly reveals his gift for exposing women's pettiness and jealousy. He wrote this scene of three women confronting one another with complete detachment, with no attempts to cover up their naked dislikes. The dialogue transcends mere cattiness and develops into well-bred bitchiness, and the chapter is a triumph of understanding of the feminine soul. It stands high on the list of the best scenes in Munro's writings, although it is unpleasant enough to read.

After her marriage, Elaine gradually realized on her honeymoon in Vienna that Courtenay Youghal had much the same selfishness as Comus, and that he was, moreover, the possessor of an attribute Comus did not have—driving ambition. Elaine had obviously not made a very happy marriage after all. Munro makes one observer of this honeymoon say: "At least Courtenay saved her from making the greatest mistake she could have made—marrying that young Bassington." "He has also," said Mrs. Goldbrook [the other observer] "helped her to make the next biggest mistake of her life—marrying Courtenay Youghal." [4]

As for Comus, his position in London, because he insisted upon leading a penniless yet extravagant life, became so untenable that he agreed to go out to a job which one of his uncles had procured for him in Africa. Comus was not enthusiastic about the prospect of being self-supporting in that unhealthy climate—in a place, as he told his mother, that would prove to be an "oubliette" —and he did not appear at all grateful for the opportunity to forward the civilizing influence of the British Empire. Francesca gave a farewell dinner party for Comus, a dinner party which, far from being happy, was almost a disaster. Munro, by many touches, gave to this dinner a feeling of impending death for Comus.

A chapter is then devoted to a description of Comus' unenthusiastic attempts at performing his job in steaming West Africa, but his duties and the nature of his employment are not detailed. Munro drew upon his own experiences when he had been a youngster in Burma to show how deeply Comus resented his involuntary exile, and how much he regretted the loss of the glamorous life in England and nostalgically longed for the fleshpots of London's West End. Munro had served in a tropical backwater of the British Empire in 1893, and judging by the bitter recollection in *The Unbearable Bassington,* it was not a happy memory.[5] The self-pity discernible in this picture of poor Comus Bassington's fate belies the frequent statements Munro made of his intention to retire to the wilds of Siberia. This is an incredible concept: Munro could never have been absorbed and creative anywhere but at the fountainhead in England of his own little world, in spite of his acid criticism and growing alienation from it—the milieu of fashion, wealth, and power.

At the book's end, Francesca received a preliminary notice that Comus was extremely ill in West Africa, a notice which from its ominous wording caused her in her misery to walk blindly through the parks at London's center, recognizing at last that she loved her son more than her comfortable way of life, or even her household possessions. This chapter has been cited as a prime example of Munro's ability to write evocatively about spiritual suffering and his masterly creation of an aura of aching and pervasive misery. And this chapter is good evidence that Munro was always aware of the basic sadness and universal sorrow of existence, in spite of his flippancy and the somewhat sour humor that has come to be his trademark.

Stoically, Francesca on her unseeing walk gradually resigned herself to learning the worst about Comus' illness; and, when she dully returned to her beloved house in Mayfair, she was given a second cablegram which reported the death of Comus. And within the hour a report came from a visiting art expert who pronounced that the Van der Meulen painting which held the place of honor in her drawing room was not authentic, merely an excellent copy. This final touch to Munro's theme was perhaps gratuitous; and, instead of deepening the sense of sadness, it is in actuality too shattering, too cruel, to put on top of the events which had gone on before.

II *Unpleasant, But a* Succès D'estime

The Unbearable Bassington was published in October, 1912 under the artistically impeccable and socially correct aegis of John Lane. This first novel of Munro's was quite well received critically, although in most instances the reviewers were surprised by its innate sadness, where they had expected a book-long demonstration of "Saki's" wit. Munro's own feelings were mixed, for Ethel records: "Opinion varied very much about the book—one friend whom Hector asked for a candid opinion, said it was unbalanced, this Hector rather thought himself." [6]

Among certain of the literati, this book evoked something of an effect of startled approbation. Hugh Walpole wrote of this effect: "I can remember very vividly the shock of surprise that 'The Unbearable Bassington' gave . . . that extraordinary book, certainly one of the most curious and unusual works in modern English literature, but it was with the publication of that novel that the world began to perceive 'Reginald' as merely a mask that had disguised him [Munro] from too curious persons." [7]

There is an obvious intent to convey an effect of impending, self-induced doom in the style and in the cumulative construction of this book; and, for all its digressions and its discursiveness, the novel does impart a feeling of portentousness and sinister inexorability that is a tribute to Munro's writing skill. He conveyed his motif of preordained misfortune, of impending disaster, in an ever-thickening atmosphere of nightmare inevitability. One way in which he did so was to surround most of the characters in the book with an air of pessimism; they have a black outlook which is sensed even in their funniest observations. Munro had his character Lady Veula Croot say these words about the ending of a play: "Of course, one can foresee the end; she will come to her husband with the announcement that their longed-for child is going to be born, and that will smooth over everything. So conveniently effective, to wind up a comedy with the commencement of some one else's tragedy. And everyone will go away saying 'I'm glad it had a happy ending.'" [8]

The darkness of the atmosphere is everywhere lighted up by the infernal flashes of Munro's little writing touches, like Comus' seeing a dog which appeared to members of his family only when they were about to die, or the chilling description of Francesca's portrait in a painting called *Harvest.* Munro maintained this sense of foreboding and hopelessness throughout the book. *The Unbearable Bassington* is, therefore, an unpleasant, unsettling, and disturbing book; but its repellent theme and unsympathetic attitudes are typical of Munro's acceptance of the harshness of life and of his disillusioned view of the inconsistencies and failures of human nature. Munro was not a writer to sugar-coat his material in order to spare his readers' sensibilities; his talents lay in the opposite direction; and, whenever possible, although in the greatest good taste, he called a spade a bloody shovel.

Almost without exception the book's analysts admonished the reader not to overlook the real tragedy of the story, which is the mother's belated awakening to maternal love, rather than the son's death in exile. It was by its theme and its treatment a book intended, like Munro's short stories, for the wealthy and leisured, the washed and anointed, and its reception in this class's periodicals—the *Morning Post,* the *Bystander,* the *Outlook*—was sympathetic and understanding. To the privileged people toward whom it was slanted the story of *The Unbearable Bassington* was indeed a tragedy.

But Munro's attempt to make the fate of Comus Bassington into a "raw deal," something grossly unfair, a tragedy, does not stand up to the test of modern values. Many sons of the Establishment were "sent out" to earn a living in the unhealthier reaches of the British Empire; and many wild young men of this class, the black sheep and scapegraces like Comus Bassington, who were actually paid to stay from their respectable families in the home island, became "remittance men." It was not an unusual situation, and certainly Bassington's story was not tragedy.

There were sights, sounds, and events in London, right under Munro's nose, which were truly tragic: the unfortunates who had to spend their nights on the Embankment, the pavement artists, the cab touts, the tuberculars crowded into the warrens of the slums, the pageant of hunger, poverty, and ignorance that daily paraded through the city. Here was the stuff of real tragedy, tragedy of a scope and intensity never achieved in Munro's little book —a book whose characters, by contrast, underwent piffling misadventures, these characters who had enough to eat and wear, and facilities for keeping themselves clean and warm, and who had been given the inestimable advantages of an education.

The Unbearable Bassington never went into complete eclipse. Discriminating readers who admired immaculately written novels with unusual themes kept the book alive—often barely alive—over the years. The book had also a certain snob appeal and quite a few of the British literati made a point of being familiar with *The Unbearable Bassington* and with its characters.[9] In 1947 the book was translated into French by Raymond Asselin as *L'Insupportable Bassington,* with footnotes explaining the exotic customs and traditions of the British upper classes in the early 1900's. This belated translation is quite appropriate; *The Unbearable Bassington* is very French in conception and execution, with its lack of sentimentality, brittle wit, and clear-eyed view of humanity. Munro would have been pleased.

III *An Expanded Version of "Saki-ism"*

In this novel may be found almost all of the subjects, opinions, and mannerisms that Munro had hitherto injected separately into his shorter fiction; among his major enthusiasms only his militarism is missing. It is as though he had pulled together all the strings of his writing talent when he composed the book.

Maurice Baring, in his Introduction to *The Unbearable Bassington* in the collected edition, seems to have sensed that Munro was making an energetic attempt to write a really distinctive and worthy contribution to contemporary letters. Baring's Introduction, published in 1926, is also interesting for the manner in which it accepts, fourteen years after the book was published, its still contemporaneous nature by not consigning it to a vanished prewar world:

> It is . . . I think, the most interesting, because the most serious and most deeply felt, just as from a literary point of view, it is likewise

the most "important" because the most artistically executed of his books. It is a tragic story; and it might have deserved as a work of art a still higher place . . . had there been in the book—for the *story* is as tragic as possible—a stronger dose of that without which a tragedy is not a tragedy: pity. But in the category of books that deal with the misfits, failures, misunderstandings and the minor victims of misunderstandings it is a masterpiece.[10]

Although Baring found some degree of pity by Munro for his characters, he did not find enough of it to "sweeten the bitterness of the misery." Baring did find, however, a brilliant display of all of the facets of Munro's writing talent evident in the earlier "Saki" books, so that Baring could agree with the critics he quoted that *The Unbearable Bassington* was "clever, brilliant, ironic, witty, sombre, elegant, grim."

Baring credited Munro with the ability to draw and create characters vividly, to make them credible and alive—"men, women, children and even animals"—but he felt that Munro was at his best when he depicted the people of his own class, "county" families and denizens of Mayfair and Belgravia. In any case, said Baring, Munro drew his characters with a fundamental understanding of human nature; more than this, he had a great wisdom which he showed again and again in his attitude toward the predicaments of his characters. In making these observations Baring has touched on two of Munro's least-known qualities: his really broad knowledge of humanity and human nature, and his shrewdness or, rather, wisdom—qualities which are all the more disconcerting because of the usual critical pigeonholing of Munro as a great wit and purveyor of lighthearted nonsense. Baring seemed rather surprised that Munro was able to impart to this book a pervasive sadness while at the same time he was so prodigal with his wit, a wit, said Baring, "that has had time to turn to tinsel but has not been tarnished."

In *The Unbearable Bassington* Munro was developing, sharpening, perfecting his principal literary weapon, his inimitable wit, which he wielded to demonstrate his disapproval of the society world, and of the ways in which it constricted and deformed its denizens. His outlook was becoming noticeably darker now, his disenchantment with the ways of this world more pronounced, his misanthropy almost savage, although his use of his gift of wittiness did not reach its ultimate effectiveness until he employed it as a philippic against the entrenched, powerful people of Britain's controlling classes in *When William Came*. But, in this first novel, he was not at all taken with the characters of England's Best People; and at every opportunity he indicated by his cutting wit his distaste for all of them. Nobody comes off well in the periodic trials of loyalty, strength of character, and steadfastness throughout the book, thoroughly in keeping with Munro's revelation of the pettiness, stupidity, boredom, and smugness abounding in the world of the Establishment.

Maurice Baring, since he was of Munro's own class, felt that the story of Comus Bassington's fate was indisputably a tragedy, and not just one of many similar episodes in the governing of the Empire. As in Munro's novel, so in Baring's Introduction, there is no slightest indication of a realization of the theoretical wrongness of imperialism; the sins and injustices of this institution are accepted as being sanctioned by immutable laws of nature.

In the 1940's the Century Library, published by Eyre & Spottiswoode, resurrected some of the English novels of the Edwardian era which it considered to have fallen into undeserved neglect. This Century Library series reprinted *The Unbearable Bassington* in 1947, together with an Introduction by Evelyn Waugh. Writing as the veteran composer of many novels, Waugh was not quite happy about Munro's technical ability:

> As a work of art *The Unbearable Bassington* is inferior to the best of the short stories; faults in construction, which are the more disconcerting by contrast with the high skill of the writing, betray the first novel . . . The life of the book is lived within conventions more of the stage than of letters and already antiquated in 1912—the complete exclusion of sex, for instance—which strain the apparatus of illusion. It is, however, with all its manifest defects a curiously interesting book.
>
> Here, for the only time, "Saki" offers, instead of the cut gardenia, the tree flowering in its pot, still the product of the hothouse, artificially nurtured, but a complete growth, leaf, stem, root, mould and all. . . .

Waugh felt that the novel was really about the tragedy of the mother, Francesca, rather than the tragedy of her son; that Francesca's obsession with her home and its furnishings (a theme brilliantly developed a decade later by George Kelly in his play

Craig's Wife) led to a repudiation of the love-life for which she was still young enough at forty, and to a taste for footling pleasures—"bridge, the theatre and a succession of small luncheon and dinner parties" and the friendship of bores and "the dreariest people in London." The colorless people who surrounded her, said Waugh, had so atrophied Francesca that she had forgotten that livelier and more attractive people still existed.

To further his theory that Munro drew Comus Bassington as a foil and as a mirror for his mother, Waugh remarked that Comus was merely sketched in by Munro—"We really know nothing of him"—and cited the rather underdrawn way in which he, apparently friendless and unappealing, is shown attending a first night or entering his club. Waugh contemptuously minimized Comus' bills at tailors and card tables and claimed that in real life Comus would have been initiated into sex and generally "educated" by one of his mother's contemporaries, "but within the peculiar conventions in which the book is conceived, Comus must at once marry an heiress or perish. . . . Heiresses are not captured by good looking, self-centered boys fresh from school, but by men, of any age and appearance, who have learned from women the art of pleasing."

Waugh is also borne out in his observation that *The Unbearable Bassington* suffers from "faulty construction." For instance, the book repeats incidents that are completely irrelevant to the main theme; subplots that never reappear after their introductions, such as the already discussed description of Courtenay Youghal's breaking off an old affair with a rather impecunious girl so that he might marry the heiress, or Elaine's chapter-length encounter with the stranded adventurer Tom Keriway, who is a sort of Munrovian self-portrait. This discursiveness stigmatizes *The Unbearable Bassington* in a way that Munro was quick to complain of in other writers, so that the novel, unlike some of his short stories, could never be held up as a model for the beginning writer. Munro obviously was more interested here in writing about the witlessness of the society world and the interplay of the strained relationship between Comus and his mother than he was in literary craftsmanship. Still, with more rewriting, he could have made his novel much more coherent, and have thereby avoided the criticism that the book "was unbalanced." Waugh also criticized the brevity of *The Unbearable Bassington* because it is really too short for a novel. To Waugh, Munro's "one difficulty seems to have been length," and his plots were sometimes "unduly expanded." But, said Waugh:

> The defects of the book have been remarked; its virtues are abundant and delectable. "Saki" stands in succession between Wilde and Firbank in the extinct line of literary dandies. The wit is continuous and almost unfailing. . . . "Saki" has attempted and achieved a *tour de force* in limiting himself to the most commonplace material in its most commonplace aspect, in eschewing all the eccentrics which come so easily to English humourists, and the strong passions which are foundations of satire, and producing a work that is wholly brilliant.[11]

IV *Sexuality by Indirection*

Possibly because he was writing from the more up-to-date vantage point of 1947, Waugh made several pertinent observations that had escaped earlier analysts of the book. It is true, for instance, that in *The Unbearable Bassington* Munro played down or elided sexual influences and manifestations in a story based in great part on sexual attraction. Munro was writing for a 1912 readership, one which placed great import on superficial respectability, and to have written anything which might be construed as improper would have alienated Munro's very proper and respectable audience. At that time there did not exist the very great freedom in writing about sex which is universal today, and reticence in this matter was *not* a convention that Waugh described as "already antiquated in 1912."

Munro, in at least his regard for the proprieties, was a Victorian writer. He was a man of thirty at Queen Victoria's death, and he had also been born and bred in the atmosphere of genteel repression of animality which is the hallmark of Victoria's reign. He neither wished to be nor could he have been more explicit about aspects of sex in his writing. His readers were equally reticent; in this worship of superficial respectability, no matter how hypocritical, they were proper Victorians all.

Ingvar Andersson, Munro's Swedish critic, has suggested that a psychiatric examination of Munro's work by someone trained in both psychoanalysis and the creation of fiction would be very fruitful. It may be conceded without the psychoanalysis that Munro was a mass of complexes—he chose the Oedipal relationship as the main theme of *The Unbearable Bassington*—although that expression and other now familiar terms of Freudian jargon were then almost unknown—but never could he have brought himself to write baldly about sexuality, clever though he was at introducing its phenomena obliquely. Munro's theme of the mother-son relationship in *The Unbearable Bassington* is the mirrored obverse of his own personal history. Because of his early loss of his mother he never experienced love from her, or had the opportunity of extending his own to her. He seems to have chosen this Oedipus theme innocently for its relatively unhackneyed nature and with no premeditation of shocking his basically conventional readership by its unhealthy overtones.

There are many hints and rather open suggestions of sexual incidents throughout *The Unbearable Bassington* if the book is examined for them, but still it is apparent what Waugh meant by his remark about "the complete exclusion of sex." Munro always wrote in a reticent manner about this most basic of topics, and though he was forced to deal with it, however gingerly, in *The Unbearable Bassington,* he almost invariably avoided it in his fiction. Was it natural reticence, distaste, or downright ignorance of the subject? Whatever the reason, the absence of this subject is another of the characteristics of Munro's writing, which is more the pity, because an occasional dollop of sexuality would have made his work all the more plausible and delectable.

V *Taken from the Life*

The Unbearable Bassington is also something of a *roman à clef.* Some of the more readily identifiable individuals, social, political, and literary celebrities of the day, whom Munro rather thinly disguised in his book, take the perceptive reader back to that period when these people were the cynosure of the newspaper-reading public. The Reverend Vaughan, the real-life divine who drew large segments of the upper crust into his church by his series of castigating sermons on the subject "The Sins of Society," was presented by Munro as "Canon Besomley . . . the big preaching man." Munro wrote: " 'I've been to hear him scold the human race once or twice,' said Francesca. . . . 'The sort of popular pulpiteer who spanks the vices of his age, and lunches with them afterwards,' said Lady Caroline." [12]

Elinor Glyn, the good-looking writer whose novel *Three Weeks* had been a recent and scandalous success appeared as the authoress of a book called *The Woman Who Wished it Was Wednesday.* Munro wrote of her: "It used to be the convention that women writers should be plain and dowdy; now we have gone to the other extreme and built them on extravagantly decorative lines. . . . She looks as if she might have created the world in six days and destroyed it on the seventh." [13] Another literary light of that day, and one whom Munro disliked, Bernard Shaw, appears in this book as "Sherard Blaw, the dramatist who had discovered himself, and who had given so ungrudgingly of his discovery to the world." [14] It is difficult to say which of two men, Bernard Shaw or David Lloyd George, was the greater of Munro's bugaboos; whatever the choice, Munro never missed an opportunity to sneer in print at these two reformers.

The character of Courtenay Youghal resembles in wit, dandyism, and Conservative political persuasion the F. E. Smith type of that day's rising young politician. And Munro, of course, gave the character Courtenay Youghal many of his own best lines to say—lines that belittled and ridiculed the incumbent Liberal government. Sir Edward Roan, Munro's pseudonym for Sir Edward Grey, the Foreign Secretary, is the subject of a conversation at a card party; and Munro has some of his women characters make his own sharp comments on the then contemporary political scene. His observations are very wittily expressed, but surely women, even women of the wealthy, leisured stratum, would not take such an overriding interest in politics and politicians as Munro made them display. Munro wrote of Grey:

> Francesca was a Ministerialist by family interest and allegiance, and was inclined to take up the cudgels at the suggested disparagement aimed at the Foreign Secretary.
>
> "He amuses me so much" purred Lady Caroline. . . .
>
> "Really? He has been rather a brilliant success at the Foreign Office, you know," said Francesca.
>
> "He reminds one so of a circus elephant—infinitely more intelligent than the people who direct him, but quite content to go on putting his foot down or taking it up as may be required, quite unconcerned whether he steps on a meringue or a hornet's nest in the process of going where he's expected to go."
>
> "How can you say such things?" protested Francesca.
>
> "I can't," said Lady Caroline; "Courtenay Youghal said it in the

House last night . . . some of the things he says have just enough truth behind them to redeem them from being merely smart; for instance, his summing up of the Government's attitude towards our embarrassing Colonial Empire in the wistful phrase 'happy is the country that has no geography.' "

"What an absurdly unjust thing to say," put in Francesca; "I daresay some of our Party at some time have taken up that attitude, but everyone knows that Sir Edward is a sound Imperialist at heart." [15]

Without once mentioning the party labels of Liberal and Conservative, Munro made clear *his* choice between them. And Munro sketched in Grey with, for him, an atypical respect for a member of the Liberal party, undoubtedly because Grey was so obviously a gentleman born and bred, and possibly, too, because Grey was a dedicated bird-watcher and nature lover, both fine attributes in Munro's eyes.

The card party scene continued in its mounting political bitterness with the remark of Lady Caroline Benaresq:

". . . no one would be rash enough to insure a politician against heart failure. Particularly when he happens to be in office."

"Anyhow, I don't see that the Opposition leaders would have acted any differently in the present case," said Francesca.

"One should always speak guardedly of the Opposition leaders," said Lady Caroline, in her gentlest voice; "one never knows what a turn in the situation may do for them."

"You mean they may one day be at the head of affairs?" asked Serena briskly.

"I mean they may one day lead the Opposition. One never knows." [16]

VI *The Tory View of Politics*

This constantly recurring aspect of Munro's writing, his engrossment in the mechanics of British politics at the highest level, almost dominates his black-sheep theme in *The Unbearable Bassington.* Most of the figures in the book have some sort of political background. Henry Greech, Francesca's brother, was a Member of Parliament. Sir Julian Jull, another M.P., had been knighted and appointed governor of one of the British West Indian islands by the Liberal party; and Francesca found Sir Julian to be poor company indeed: "When she took tea on the Terrace of the House she was wont to lapse into rapt contemplation of St. Thomas's Hospital whenever she saw him within bowing distance." [17] In this passage there is an excellent indication of the proprietary attitude of the Establishment toward Parliament.

Munro, all through this book, introduced technical and sometimes clinical discussions of Parliamentary maneuvers and intrigues; it is almost as if his main theme of the scapegrace got away from him and the subject of politics became dominant. He himself had the common proprietary attitude toward politics, a trait which seems to have been characteristic of both the Liberal and Conservative paladins active in society. It mattered not too much to which party one belonged; the principal thing was to have the correct birth, background, schooling, and accent. And, because Munro was writing for this level, he had the honesty to write as a snob, snobbishly, and to portray the superiority in all respects of the wealthy, well-bred caste. He believed in this superiority with the deepest conviction; and, whenever he had occasion to introduce the lower orders into his plot, he mentioned them impersonally, like articles of furniture, as if they—the footmen, the maids, the crossing sweepers—were expected to be discreetly present whenever their services were needed.

And the political privilege and preferment of this upper world were taken for granted, too. Comus was proposed and accepted as secretary to Sir Julian Jull, who in turn had been made the governor of an island in the British West Indies. They were both gentlemen, and so, in Munro's eyes, their unimpeded progress up the ladder of imperial opportunity must be accepted as an intrinsic right. *The Unbearable Bassington* is permeated with this unconsciously arrogant assumption of the superiority and deserved preferment of the wealthy and well-bred stratum. Once again, one marvels at the detachment of convinced Liberal John Lane in publishing Munro's work.

And yet, for all Munro's mastery of his society milieu, there is a curious lack of verisimilitude in *The Unbearable Bassington,* an absence of realism in the presentation of how the Best People really spent their daily lives. True, the attitudes, beliefs, and opinions of these people are set down credibly enough; Munro spent most of his life in their company, and their opinions and attitudes were also his. But somehow the reader does not quite believe in the authenticity of Munro's characters. It is as if Munro had had a thesis to expound, as if he could not be bothered to make the characters who illustrated it into flesh-and-blood creations.

VII *A Foreshadowing of Future Books*

Before the publication of *The Unbearable Bassington,* Munro's short stories had been the only guide to his ability as a writer; now there was a novel to give a full-length mirroring of his talent. Now, too, the readers of *The Unbearable Bassington* could see in panoramic form Munro's deeply pessimistic view of life and his very considerable, if jaundiced, knowledge of people set forth bluntly and shrewdly in a bald tale of human folly. Now it was also plain that Munro was not after all basically a humorist with the funny man's comfortably indulgent outlook on the world. He was a writer honest in his pessimism and unblinking in his repelled regard of humanity, a most original and disturbing writer.

As a guide to what Munro might have accomplished in the field of English fiction had he lived longer, *The Unbearable Bassington* is quite revealing. The book has an almost tangible striving for distinction that is indicative of some really fresh, absorbing, and no doubt unsettling books to follow. If Munro's attitudes and gifts had survived to live in the disillusioned postwar period of the 1920's they would unquestionably have produced some of the most amusing and penetrating books of a disillusioned era.

CHAPTER 7

The Novelist as Propagandist

DURING the years from 1900 to 1914 the theme of a military attack by Imperial Germany upon the British Isles was quite popular with British writers: it appeared in several novels, in magazine serials, in a play, and even in cartoons. The great British public seemed to sense the latent threat of the military power of the country just across from them on the North Sea, for any book that dealt with a projection of German aggression against England could be assured a morbid but widespread success. This general belief in the inevitability of a British-German war seems startlingly prescient now, but in the first decade of this century the British public felt, smugly perhaps, that if and when such a war came the British fleet and their homeland's very insularity would give them sufficient protection.

One of the first books on this subject to receive a popular reception was Erskine Childers' *The Riddle of the Sands* (1903) which told of a fleet of German invasion barges lurking in a remote section of the German North Sea coast, waiting for the propitious moment to attack an unsuspecting England. Most British readers seemed to regard the novel as a sort of science fiction work, a fantasy beyond all probability; and they did not react with any degree of alarm to its warning. Thenceforward, books treating of this German invasion theme were published by authors of varying degrees of writing skill. William le Quex offered the British mass mind *The Great Invasion of 1910,* Henry Curties published *When England Slept,* and even the boy's magazine *Chums* joined the jeremiad chorus by publishing in 1913 a serial called *The Swoop of the Eagle: A Story of the German Invasion.*

But it was a play, *An Englishman's Home,* by Major Guy du Maurier, produced in the winter of 1909, that caused the greatest stir and provoked the most probing discussions of the subject of a German invasion.[1] *An Englishman's Home* showed an English family reacting—and reacting badly—to an invasion by the Germans (perfunctorily disguised as "Nearlanders" in the play) of the English east coast. In the entre' actes of the melodrama the audiences absorbedly discussed du Maurier's story of unprepared Englishmen trying to repel an invasion of well-armed, professional military.

An ultimate British victory was specified or implied in all of these stories, but Munro, with his determined originality, postulated *his* entry into the cycle on a swift, total and probably irretrievable defeat of England by Germany; he confronted his readers in his second novel with the awful picture of a beaten England incapable of muddling through this catastrophe. Munro had no "stout fella" stoicism or sugar-coated optimism to proffer his readers in the writing of his second novel, *When William Came.* Munro did not write his prophecy of doom with any thought that his book would reach a mass audience, the ruck, the vast majority of Englishmen; they could not possibly have been alarmed by Munro's book—they could not even have comprehended the newspapers for which he wrote. Munro, rather, aimed his book at the relatively few people in Britain who wielded power. The intention of *When William Came* was to disturb and to alert these truly influential people.

I *A Putative British Nightmare*

The plot line of *When William Came* is rather slapdash, written as though Munro really was less interested in literary carpentry than in ringing all the changes possible on the consequences of an English defeat by the Germans. Munro's indifference to careful plotting is so obvious, in fact, that more than one of the book's reviewers called it, with some justification, a collection of dialogues about the causes of England's defeat. The story line of the novel, apart from the central event of Britain's defeat by Germany, is rather improbable; and in places it is downright unbelievable.

Murrey Yeovil, the "hero" or protagonist of *When William Came,* is that typical Munrovian creation, a wealthy young man of the upper classes. Yeovil was far from home, hunting in the wilds of Siberia, when England was swiftly defeated by Germany. Yeovil had been very ill from malaria; but, when he learned of his country's defeat, he doggedly beat his way back to his sumptuous home in London. Here he was reunited with his wife Cicely, who was wealthy in her own right, and his partner in a marriage of convenience. Yeovil demonstrated a remarkable tolerance for the amorous intrigues of his wife, who consoled herself during his absences from England with a succession of good-looking young men.

Cicely immediately set about the newly returned Yeovil's education in how to conduct himself as a German subject; she called in an old friend of Yeovil's, a Doctor Holham, who told Yeovil the details of England's defeat by Germany. The next morning, his second one back in England, Yeovil learned from the personal experiences of a walk around central London of the Teutonic discipline imposed upon the formerly carefree Londoners by the German overlords.

A dialogue follows between two of the German conquerors in a London café, in which they discuss the possibilities of the Britons' ever rising to throw the German masters out of the island. Munro, with many shrewd comments on the English and German national characters, made the point that, even if the British won a temporary liberation from the Germans, the Germans would be back in the island as conquerors within three weeks because *they* now controlled the seas and could blockade the British Isles to the point of starvation. Munro may have skimped the description of the fighting and the war in which he postulated Germany's defeat of England, but he gave a plausible and vivid picture of the thoroughness of the German control of England and the futility of any English resistance.

As Yeovil grew more accustomed to this new way of life in England, he became indignant and then disgusted by the adjustments, conformities, and acquiescences which the people of his own social level were making to the German occupation. He attended a first night presentation of the "suggestion dancing" of one of his wife's protégées, Gorla Mustleford, and found the performance to be crude and childish. He was repelled and disgusted by the enthusiastic reception a group of wealthy Britons gave to Gorla Mustleford's "dancing"; these people had chosen to remain on under the Germans to try to continue London's aforetime society whose better elements had gone into voluntary exile.

Then England's German rulers published an Imperial decree which excused all Britons from compulsory military service in the

German armed forces since, the decree stated with mocking suavity, the British had traditionally rejected the sacrifices of military conscription as being beneath them. German troops would do any fighting necessary to protect the British Isles, and Britons were forbidden to bear arms. Of course, the British would have to pay very stiff taxes for this military shield.

At that point, Yeovil started on a pilgrimage to a place he sensed would have made no concessions to the German conquest. His train journey through rural England was written by Munro to point up both the beauty of the landscape and the shame of having lost it to an alien conqueror. Yeovil's fellow passenger in the railway carriage was a Hungarian, who thought Yeovil to be another alien in England. With this loosening of restraint, the Hungarian wonderingly dwelt upon the average Englishman's carelessness and complacency in allowing the Germans to conquer such an attractive and formerly virile country.

After the Hungarian had left the train, his place in Yeovil's carriage was taken by an Englishman of the unfeeling, rather stupid type that resisted the German overlordship solely with its loud mouth. Munro wrote of this fellow: "a patriot who had never handled a rifle, or mounted a horse or pulled an oar, but who had never flinched from demolishing his country's enemies with his tongue." [2]

Yeovil finally ended his journey at Torywood, a "stately home" which was the country seat of old Lady Eleanor Greymarten, an uncompromising nationalist who had always been active in politics.[3] This old woman's steadfast opposition to the German conquest of England was in startling contrast to Gorla Mustleford's artistic and social accommodation to the German masters—a contrast all the more ironic because Gorla Mustleford was Lady Eleanor's granddaughter. The old lady fervently asked Yeovil not to submit supinely to the German conquerors.

Next, Ronnie Starr, who was Cicely Yeovil's current paramour, achieved a sudden success as a pianist and left Cicely for the patronage of more influential women. Ronnie seems to be Munro's symbol for the archetype of the collaborator, the conscienceless opportunist who used his country's disastrous fall to promote his career.

Munro's own devout clubmanship is next worked into the book.[4] The "hero," Yeovil, rashly joined one of the clubs which had sprung up under the influence of the German occupiers; but, when he went to inspect it, he found it to be untenable. This club, "the Cartwheel," was, Munro wrote, "a blend of the railway station at Cologne, the Hotel Bristol in any European capital, and the second act in most musical comedies." [5] Munro was attempting to depict the dissolution of the standards of the old ruling classes of England, and the enthusiastic acceptance of the new German masters by the British collaborators who now represented the Best People in England.

The scene then moved to India, which the Germans had allowed the British to retain as a colony. Here Munro gave his version of the everyday life of a family of British émigrés who in India could remain loyal to the old British flag without German interference. This chapter allowed Munro to contrast the lot of many upper-class British émigrés who had to put up with many deprivations and hardships in the colonies with the despicable ease and wealth of those complaisant Britons who had remained on in the home island. In the writing of this chapter, Munro's patriotism can be seen to have been very fervid—overidealized and oversimplified, perhaps, but fervid.

Back in England, Murrey Yeovil succumbed step by step to the fact of the German conquest by taking up again the allurements of English "county" life, the leisured and privileged life in which he had been brought up, a round of fox hunting, riding, and shooting. Yeovil's wife Cicely, a most plausible sophist and born collaborationist, insidiously helped him to adopt a hopeless resignation. Besides, his original determination to be a resistor to the German rule was sapped by his physical weakness and finally drained away through an unsuspected weakness of character: his seduction by the entangling charms of a country squire's life. Surprisingly, though, Yeovil through his quotation of a bellicose quatrain of Cowper, inspired one of the young favorites of London society, Tony Luton, to give up his sybaritic existence and go to sea as a deckhand on a Canadian freighter.

Finally, after a costume ball in London at which the German conquerors and the English natives hobnob in an atmosphere of progressive reconciliation, a procession of Boy Scouts, which was to march past the German Emperor in Hyde Park as a demonstration of Germany's assimilation of the English, never appeared for the review. Munro seemed to think that the Boy Scouts, by perpetrating this act of defiance, typified the spirit of resistance in the younger generation of Britons, and so the book ends on a note of hopefulness.

II *As a Patriotic Service*

In writing *When William Came* Munro had two purposes in mind: he wanted to make his own contribution to the cause of instituting universal military training in Great Britain, and he wanted to startle and shock the influential people of England out of their smugness and false sense of security by alerting them to the looming German menace. He undertook the job with all the seriousness and determination that underlay his superficial cynicism. His purposeful approach to composing the book is apparent in Ethel's comment on *When William Came:* "Hector wrote part of it while staying with me near Rye, and in order to get absolute quiet spent hours writing in a wood near." [6] Even the chapter headings of *When William Came* are used as instruments of Munro's purpose; the chapters are not divided by chaste numerals, as in *The Unbearable Bassington,* but are satirical descriptions of the distasteful material each chapter treats of; and they become progressively more sardonic in their wording as one approaches the end of the book.

When Munro's sincerity was put to the proof less than a year after the publication of the book, he immediately volunteered for the army after the outbreak of war in August, 1914. And of this incident Ethel wrote: "Hector told a friend that, having written 'When William Came,' he ought to go half-way to meet him." [7]

It does not seem to have been Munro's intention to make money out of writing on a sensational theme; rather, he wrote his book in the spirit of discharging a public service, a patriotic duty. John Lane, in publishing this second novel of Munro's, must have realized that he was helping Munro to propagandize a militaristic point of view which was not very widely held by the Liberals, Lane's political persuasion. Yet Lane obviously foresaw that the book would be given a good critical reception because of the topicality of its theme, while it would appeal to the small but assured circle of "Saki" enthusiasts.

In writing *When William Came,* Munro was attempting to furnish some ammunition to one segment of British opinion—usually the opinion of the most dogmatically militaristic type, though sometimes the opinion of calmer and more objective people—that favored peacetime universal military conscription of all the able-bodied young men of Great Britain in the same manner that countries of the Continent conscripted their youth. This innovation would give Great Britain a large standing army; and the country would not, in time of emergency, have to rely on the extremely capable but tiny regular army and the half-trained Territorial troops. The formation of a large well-trained British army seemed to these advocates (and to Munro) to be a wise precaution to take against any possible attack by a European power.

Yet there were a few in Britain who minimized the possibility of any German aggression. This scoffing attitude was reflected in a series of cartoons by Heath Robinson, a sort of British Rube Goldberg, which appeared during the spring and summer of 1910 in the magazine *Sketch.* This series, published under the heading "Incidents of the Coming German Invasion of England," represented the German soldiers as a collection of clumsy and comically gullible oafs who were easily mastered by the amateur defenders of England and the volunteer part-time soldiers of the Territorials. Munro undoubtedly saw this series of cartoons, and he was undoubtedly infuriated by the ridiculing of the German soldiery in them. A realistic idea of Germany's military potential could never have been derived from the examples of the Germans resident in England, who were rather meek specimens, usually menials like waiters and street musicians. *When William Came* was Munro's riposte to just this sort of pooh-poohing of a very real threat.

Although skepticism about the possibility of a great war was quite commonly entertained by British and European intellectuals until the events of August, 1914, disabused them, a few believed that the holocaust was inevitable. In Britain, many of the advocates of peacetime conscription were, of course, extreme reactionaries whose militarism complemented their resistance to any reforms in industry or in the social system, but there were more disinterested advocates, too. The man who personified the movement to institute peacetime conscription was Lord Roberts, the general who had finally brought the Boer War to an end. He acknowledged Munro's contribution of *When William Came* in a letter to him; according to Ethel, "Lord Roberts wrote him a most appreciative note, which pleased him tremendously." [8]

Other literate Britons read Munro's warning with somewhat

less belief in the imminence of the danger. Thomas Anstey Guthrie wrote of Munro's book in his diary: "On New Year's Day [1914] I read Saki's powerful and bitter 'When William Came,' and, greatly as it impressed me, I saw it chiefly as remarkably able propaganda work for Lord Roberts's scheme, and thought a war with Germany a very remote contingency." [9]

III *Predictions True and Unmaterialized*

There are certain of Munro's imaginings and military projections which give *When William Came* an occasional oracular quality. For instance, he foresaw the overwhelming significance of air power. In a passage describing a new German club in conquered Piccadilly, the "Army Aeronaut Club," where there was a continual passage of "gay-hued uniforms, Saxon, Prussian, Bavarian, Hessian . . . through its portals," Munro wrote sardonically: "The mastering of the air and the creation of a scientific aerial war fleet, second to none in the world, was an achievement of which the conquering race was pardonably proud, and for which it had good reason to be duly thankful. Over the gateways was blazoned the badge of the club, an elephant, whale and eagle, typifying the three armed forces of the State, by land and sea and air; the eagle bore in its beak a scroll with the proud legend: 'The last am I, but not the least.'" [10]

Munro foresaw, too, the surrender of the pacifist labor parties of both Great Britain and Germany to patriotic fervor—which actually happened in 1914. "The evangel of brotherhood," he wrote forebodingly, "did not blunt a single Teuton bayonet when the hour came." [11] In one respect, however, Munro failed as a prophet: he could not project and did not imagine the barbaric harshness of an actual German occupation, the barbarity to which today most of the countries of Europe can testify. True, Munro in a startlingly prescient passage made Murrey Yeovil say of the Germans: "We have given a clever and domineering people a chance to plant themselves down as masters in our land; I don't imagine that they are going to give us an easy chance to push them out." [12]

In the civilized atmosphere of 1913 most people did not imagine that rapacity and bestiality could ever be elevated to the place of a national policy, and in the writing of *When William Came* Munro innocently projected his own innate chivalry to the behavior of Germany toward a conquered England. For a guide to Teutonic expansionism and digestive capabilities, Munro had Germany's comparatively gentlemanly behavior in Alsace-Lorraine and western Poland to study, although he did not guess at the Draconian rule Germany was to institute in Belgium from 1914 to 1918. But to alert his complacent fellow Britons, Munro could never have invented episodes on a par with the incredible realities of Lidice, Rotterdam, Auschwitz, or Ouradour-sur-Glane.

IV *How to Combine Polemic and Novel*

For one who had such a long and ramified military ancestry, and who himself was a militaristic, combative, hot-blooded man, Munro strangely enough skimped and even fudged the description of the Anglo-German war and the quick defeat of England in *When William Came.* Other contemporary writers, H. G. Wells for instance, would have made a description of such a war much more exciting and credible. It really is inexplicable that Munro did not make a greater effort at imagining and relating the details of so significant a war. Instead, Munro presents a perfunctory description of it in *When William Came:*

> It started with a wholly unimportant disagreement about some frontier business in East Africa; there was a slight attack of nerves in the stock markets, and then the whole thing seemed in a fair way towards being settled. The negotiations over the affair began to drag unduly, and there was a further flutter of nervousness in the money world. And then one morning the papers reported a highly menacing speech by one of the German Ministers, and the situation began to look black indeed. "He will be disavowed," every one said over here, but in less than twenty-four hours those who knew anything knew that the crisis was on us—only their knowledge came too late. "War between two such civilized and enlightened nations is an impossibility," one of our leaders of public opinion had declared on the Saturday; by the following Friday the war had indeed become an impossibility, because we could no longer carry it on. It burst on us with calculated suddenness and we were just not enough, everywhere where the pressure came. Our ships were good against their ships, our seamen were better than their seamen, but our ships were not able to cope with their ships plus their superiority in aircraft. Our trained men were good against their trained men, but they could not be in several places at once, and the enemy could. Our half-trained men and our untrained men could not master the science of war at a moment's notice, and a moment's notice was all they got. The enemy were a nation appren-

ticed in arms, and we were not even the idle apprentice: we had not deemed apprenticeship worth our while. There was courage enough running loose in the land, but it was like unharnessed electricity, it controlled no forces, it struck no blows. There was no time for heroism and the devotion which a drawn-out struggle, however hopeless, can produce; the war was over almost as soon as it had begun. After the reverses which happened with lightning rapidity, in the final three days of warfare, the newspapers made no effort to pretend that the situation could be retrieved; editors and public alike recognized that these were blows over the heart, and that it was a matter of moments before we were counted out. One might liken the whole affair to a snap checkmate early in a game of chess; one side had thought out the moves, and brought the requisite pieces into play, the other side was hampered and helpless, with its resources unavailable, its strategy discounted in advance. That, in a nutshell, is the history of the war.[13]

Conveniently and probably intentionally, Munro failed to mention that Great Britain had loyal colonies and populous allies to succor her, but such a point would not have helped him in expounding his thesis—the folly of not having some sort of peacetime military conscription in England. He did, however, write fleetingly and perfunctorily of the way in which Britain's allies abandoned her: "The conquerors were in a position to dictate what terms they pleased. . . . There was no European combination ready to say them nay, and certainly no one Power was going to be rash enough to step in to contest the terms of the treaty that they imposed on the conquered." [14]

V

I was playing golf the day
That the Germans landed.
All our troops had run away,
All our ships were stranded.
And the thought of England's shame
Very nearly spoiled my game.

(Music hall song by Harry Graham *circa* 1909)

The writing device most often used in *When William Came* is the illuminative-by-indirection dialogue, which Munro used throughout the book to emphasize the causes and consequences of a German victory over England. Murrey Yeovil has dialogues with a politically aware physician, a London policeman, a collaborating clubman, a Hungarian visitor to England, a combative young clergyman, and a *grande dame* of British politics. Cicely has inveigling conversations with her husband; a French naturalist converses with a British matron transplanted to India; and even a pair of German conquerors discuss the causes of English defeat and the possibility of German assimilation of the English. In all these dialogues Munro, without having to comment directly, was able to sidelight the horrible plight of defeated England and the folly of not being prepared militarily; it was an effective way of underscoring these two main issues.

At many points in the book Munro's fervor is so pronounced that it almost seems as if he had forgotten he was writing pure fiction and that he believed the German conquest of England actually to have taken place. Munro vividly conveyed his vicarious grief and shame, his haunting sense of an irretrievable loss of country. A passage describes what Yeovil saw of the English countryside from a train rolling through it, and in the context within which Munro wrote it, it is most pertinent to his technique of illuminating the cause of shame and the sorrow of loss by indirection:

> Tall grasses and meadow-weeds stood in deep shocks, field after field, between the leafy boundaries of hedge or coppice, thrusting themselves higher and higher till they touched the low sweeping branches of the trees that here and there overshadowed them. Broad streams, bordered with a heavy fringe of reed and sedge, went winding away into a green distance where woodland and meadowland seemed indefinitely prolonged; narrow streamlets lost to view in the growth that they fostered, disclosed their presence merely by the water-weed that showed in a riband of rank verdure threading the mellower green of the fields. On the stream banks moorhens walked with jerky confident steps, in the easy boldness of those who had a couple of other elements at their disposal in an emergency; more timorous partridges raced away from the apparition of the train, looking all leg and neck, like little forest elves fleeing from human encounter. And in the distance, over the tree line, a heron or two flapped away with slow measured wing-beats and an air of being bent on an immeasurably longer journey than the train that hurtled so frantically along the rails. Now and then the meadowland changed itself suddenly into orchard, with close-growing trees already showing the measure of their coming harvest, and then strawyard and farm buildings would slide into view; heavy dairy cattle, roan and skewbald and

dappled, stood near the gates, drowsily resentful of insect stings, and bunched-up companies of ducks halted in seeming irresolution between the charms of the horse-pond and the alluring neighbourhood of the farm kitchen. Away by the banks of some rushing mill-stream, in a setting of copse and cornfield, a village might be guessed at, just a hint of red roof, grey wreathed chimney and old church tower as seen from the windows of the passing train, and over it all brooded a happy, settled calm, like the dreaming murmur of a trout-stream and the far-away cawing of rooks.

It was a land where it seemed as if it must be always summer and generally afternoon, a land where bees hummed among the wild thyme and in the flower-beds of cottage gardens, where the harvest mice rustled amid the corn and nettles, and the mill-race flowed cool and silent through water-weeds and dark tunneled sluices, and made soft droning music with the wooden mill-wheel. And the music carried with it the wording of old undying rhymes, and sang of the jolly, uncaring, uncared-for miller, of the farmer who went riding upon his grey mare, of the mouse who lived beneath the merry mill-pin, of the sweet music on yonder green hill and the dancers all in yellow—the songs and fancies of a lingering olden time, when men took life as children take a long summer day, and went to bed at last with a simple trust in something they could not have explained.

Yeovil watched the passing landscape with the intent hungry eyes of a man who revisits a scene that holds high place in his affections. His imagination raced even quicker than the train, following winding roads and twisting valleys into unseen distances, picturing farms and hamlets, hills and hollows, clattering inn yards and sleepy woodlands.[15]

J. W. Lambert in his Introduction to *The Bodley Head Saki* reprints this passage with the observation that Munro had idealized the picture of the English countryside in it. Lambert concedes, though, that many Englishmen see their countryside in this more or less romantic light, and so he confirms Munro's purpose in composing this admittedly prettied-up picture: to show the British reader of 1913 what he would be losing. But Munro, the knowledgeable countryman and frequenter of fields and farmyards, could write in a much less false and bathetic manner of the English countryside. In this same book there is an excellent example of his more restrained, naturalistic manner:

The pale light of a November afternoon faded rapidly into the dusk of a November evening. Far over the countryside housewives put up their cottage shutters, lit their lamps. . . . In barnyards and poultry-runs the greediest pullets made a final tour of inspection, picking up the stray remaining morsels of the evening meal. . . . And through the cold squelching slush of a water-logged meadow a weary, bedraggled, but unbeaten fox stiffly picked his way, climbed a high bramble-grown bank, and flung himself into the sheltering labyrinth of a stretching tangle of woods. The pack of fierce-mouthed Things that had rattled him from copse and gorse-cover, along fallow and plough, hedgerow and wooded lane, for nigh on an hour, and had pressed hard on his life for the last few minutes, receded suddenly into the background of his experiences. The cold, wet meadow, the thick mask of woods, and the on-coming dusk had stayed the chase—and the fox had outstayed it. In a short time he would fall mechanically to licking off some of the mud that caked on his weary pads.[16]

From the evidence of these quotations it appears that Munro was a sincere and profound patriot with an almost aching love for his homeland, a sentiment surprising in this writer known to posterity for his jaundiced cynicism. But then his fire-eating personality accounts in large part for his hyperpatriotism. He was capable of writing in *When William Came* of "martial trappings, the swaggering joy of life, the comradeship of camp and barracks, the hard discipline of drill yard and fatigue duty, the long sentry watches, the trench digging, forced marches, wounds, cold, hunger, makeshift hospitals, and the blood-wet laurels." [17] Only an innately militaristic soul could see such things in a glamorous and joyous light.

Munro had very little knowledge of the British working class, the poor and uneducated on whom any form of universal military service would have had to fall most heavily. Whenever Munro's story line requires him to leave his own society world to enter the world of the workingman, his writing loses its authenticity of behavior and psychology; and, in fact, he disapproved of these lower orders. In his fictional picture of a British defeat he does not allow the laboring class to escape lightly:

". . . do tell me something about the poorer classes of the community. How do they take the new order of things?"

"Badly," said the young cleric . . . "one thing you may be sure of, they do not blame themselves. No true Londoner ever admits that fault lies at his door. 'No, I never!' is an exclamation that is on his lips from earliest childhood, whenever he is charged with anything blameworthy or punishable. . . . Public schoolboys and private schoolboys of the upper and middle class had their fling and took their thrashings, when they were found out, as a piece of bad luck, but 'our Bert' and 'our Sid' were of those for whom there is no condemnation; if *they* were punished it was for faults that 'no, they never' committed. Naturally the grown-up generation of Berts and Sids, the voters and householders, do not realize, still less admit, that it was they who called the tune to which the politicians danced. They had to choose between the vote-mongers and the so-called 'scare mongers,' and their verdict was for the vote-mongers all the time." [18]

Besides a lack of understanding of the lower classes, Munro here showed his contempt for their code of behavior and his disapproval of their voting overwhelmingly for the Liberal party. His was the usual Tory attitude toward the peasantry.

In composing *When William Came* Munro seemed to sense his deficiency of firsthand knowledge of the poor because he wrote mostly of the people of the upper classes whom he knew so well, against a background of fine residences in Mayfair, shooting boxes in the English countryside, the flossy world of London first nights, the clubs of St. James's. And, in fact, Munro's deepening misanthropy and his disgust with the conspicuous consumption all around him in the upper world may be plainly traced in *When William Came*. The book has unappetizing pictures of British upper-class acquiescence to domination by a foreign power in descriptions of languid young patrons of Turkish baths, of costume balls attended by the full-pursed and empty-headed, of luxury restaurants catering to fastidious epicures, of the allurements of "haberdashers', perfumers' and jewellers' show windows." The hedonism, made up of moral blindness and physical flabbiness which Munro here described as pervading the high society of London certainly would have been fertile soil for collaboration, that term which did not assume this particular and sinister connotation until World War II.

Munro's unfailingly apt and special wit is injected into the book at every opportunity, and it makes *When William Came* a frequently bewildering mixture of simple patriotic fervor and acidulous drawing-room humor. Munro's using Lady Caroline Benaresq in *The Unbearable Bassington* as the mouthpiece for his own devastating remarks is repeated in his use of Joan Mardle in *When William Came*—she who went to a costume ball as "Inconvenient Candour." Joan Mardle is made to speak Munro's own disapproving views on any form of collaboration, and to do it with wit, appropriateness, and disarming gentleness. G. K. Chesterton wrote of this tendency to cover up a deadly serious event with a jester's disguise in the makeup of Munro: "Saki was obviously very national in the fact that the very normal loyalties to which he was true were almost completely covered in public with a coat of mail of flippancy, at once as sparkling and impenetrable as the costume of a harlequin." [19]

One thread which appears consistently in this book that is distasteful to the reader of the 1960's, who has been tragically educated by the world's more recent history, is Munro's anti-Semitism, the nearly universal anti-Semitism of his caste. His intense nationalism led him to impute in *When William Came* a tendency on the part of wealthy and influential British Jews to collaborate with the German conquerors and to take the places of those of the British aristocracy who had left England. Munro did not believe that British Jews had a sufficiently deep identification with British life; the anomaly here is that even the crustiest Tory had accepted Disraeli as a true-blue Englishman and a "sound Imperialist." The emergence of Munro's anti-Semitism here, a typical Tory attitude of that day, has the appearance of his having seized an opportunity to air one of his prejudices. It certainly does nothing to amplify his theme of the necessity for military preparation in England.

Another thread in this book, and one that is the more surprising because of Munro's wide-ranging travels and his prolonged residences abroad, is his condemnation of the growing cosmopolitanism that he detected in influential artistic and political circles in England. He made the character Dr. Holham say:

> Well, you must remember that many things in modern life, especially in the big cities, are not national but international. In the world of music and art and the drama, for instance, the foreign names are legion, they confront you at every turn, and some of our British devotees of such arts are more acclimatized to the ways of Munich or Moscow than they are familiar with the life, say, of Stirling or York. For years they have lived and thought and spoken in an atmosphere and jargon of denationalized culture—even those of them who have never left our shores. They would take pains to be intimately familiar with the domestic affairs and views of life of some Galician gipsy

dramatist, and gravely quote and discuss his opinions on debts and mistresses and cookery, while they would shudder at "D'ye ken John Peel?" as a piece of uncouth barbarity.[20]

Munro seemed to be saying in *When William Came* that cosmopolitanism was potentially a threat to British purity and stability, and he wrote at length in this book of the weakening effects of cosmopolitanism on Britons wherever they halfheartedly attempted to resist their German conquerors. Narrow and perfervid nationalism, Munro seemed to think, would have helped to make the average Briton more patriotic, and therefore more amenable to peacetime conscription. At any rate, here is a most atypical instance of insularity in the writing of a usually devoted cosmopolitan. Even though Munro deplored the enervating influences of upper-class pursuits in such a terrible situation as he created in *When William Came,* his "educated scorn" and basic, underlying sympathy and identity with the "fine arts" way of life are quite obvious. Munro would have been miserable in a society made up exclusively of rude and simple patriots; he needed and sought the company of sophisticates and cosmopolitans.

When William Came subordinates novelistic art to its main, single-minded purpose: to alert an indifferent Britain to its perilous neglect of conscription. *Punch* said that the book differed from the others of its premonitory type in its callous projection of British defeat and in its depiction of the humiliations of a German occupation; but the magazine commended Munro's patriotism in writing the warning. In the literature of dire warnings *When William Came* ranks high for its almost supernatural timeliness. Uniquely personal like the contribution of the Juggler of Notre Dame, it was Munro's contribution to the cause of conscription in Great Britain.

CHAPTER 8

The Playwright of Promise

THE theater had attracted Munro from the days of his early youth, although the attraction was given no encouragement whatever in the Puritan atmosphere of Broadgate Villa. When young Munro at last escaped into the freedom of Bedford Grammar School, however, he found that singing, the recitation of poems, and the acting out of plays were compulsory and that the various "houses" of Bedford School competed among themselves to determine the best performers. Munro must have enjoyed participating in these events because he was the self-possessed type that does not go to pieces in front of an audience.

And as a young man he participated without any stage fright in the amateur theatricals which were presented in his hotel at Davos in the winter of 1892–93. "The theatricals" said Ethel, "were on a more ambitious scale than two years previously. Hector took the part of the old lawyer in 'Two Roses'; I heard an old colonel say he had created the part." [1] And, when Munro was sent to Burma in 1893, he reproached his sister, who was then enjoying the amenities of London, for not going to the theater enough: "Owl and oaf thou art," he wrote to Ethel from Burma, "not to see 'Woman of No Importance' and 'Second Mrs. T.' *The* plays of the season; what would I not give to be able to see them!" [2] The theater seems to have epitomized everything glamorous and desirable that he had left behind him in London.

When Munro began to achieve publication of his journalism and his short stories he also began to consider the stage as a possible market for his literary efforts. He strove to become a professional playwright, with his one long play, but none of his theatrical scripts achieved production during his lifetime, although three of the pieces he wrote for the stage were finally given the dignity of print in 1924 in *The Square Egg*.

I *Two Inept Curtain Raisers*

Two of these three pieces are playlets, *The Death Trap* and *Karl-Ludwig's Window,* of such brevity that their presentation even as curtain raisers would have been of debatable wisdom. They are little more than anecdotes, and much too stagy to be presented to a live audience, which might laugh in the wrong places. Munro seems to have written *The Death Trap* and *Karl-Ludwig's Window* in his late youth, before he attempted to become a professional writer, because they are certainly uncommercial, for their excess of gore and melodrama was outdated even at the turn of the century. These playlets illustrate, however, certain recurrent subjects in Munro's work in other media: his preoccupation with the blood lines and family trees of Continental royalty and nobility (Munro had his own copy of the *Almanach de Gotha*); his militarism; his admiration for the large gesture, the intransigence of youth; his deep sense of *noblesse oblige;* and a concern with death so pervasive that it can only be termed a death wish.

"The Death Trap" is extremely Graustarkian in feeling and in setting, reading almost like an excerpt from *The Prisoner of Zenda.* The playlet's characters are given as "Dmitri, reigning prince of Kadaria" and four officers of the "Kranitzki Regiment of Guards," who appear in "an antechamber in the Prince's Castle at Tzern." Three of these officers are discovered intriguing against Prince Dmitri's life, so that they may install their own man as the ruler of Kadaria. Prince Dmitri, who knows of this plot, keeps the knowledge to himself; and, when he appears on stage, he coldly dismisses the disloyal officers. Dmitri is an elegant, hard-willed youth who is sophisticated beyond his seventeen years, and who seems to represent Munro's ideal in breeding, attitudes, and upbringing.

A fourth officer of the Kranitzki Regiment, the regimental physician who is loyal to Dmitri, is told by the Prince of the deadly plot against him; and the doctor then agrees to make a false diagnosis of Dmitri's health in order to confuse the plotters. The doctor, after a supposedly spurious physical examination, tells the conspirators that Dmitri has less than six days to live. The conspirators then agree among themselves to allow Dmitri to die an imminent natural death instead of instantly murdering him; but, after they have left, the doctor announces to Dmitri that the physical examination had revealed an actual malady and that Dmitri will really die within a week.

When Dmitri commands the doctor to give him a vial of poison, the doctor agrees to his monarch's last wish and then leaves. Dmitri, who pours the vial of poison into a bottle of wine, summons the three disloyal officers to return to the royal presence. When Dmitri offers a toast to the man who will succeed him as Prince, supposedly after his natural death a week later, the disloyal officers respond to his toast, drinking the poisoned wine. All three officers die, and Dmitri himself dies immediately afterward. Munro wound up his little melodrama with about as many bodies on the stage as the final scene of *Hamlet.*

The other playlet, *Karl-Ludwig's Window,* is not quite so flamboyantly lethal: it has only one death in it, although another occurs off stage. Kurt von Jagdstein, a young officer in a cavalry regiment, serving in a country "in Eastern Europe," kills the country's Archduke in a duel over a woman. His scandalized fellow officers in the regiment give Kurt a few hours' time to kill himself, thereby expunging the disgrace of killing the Archduke. Kurt returns to his home in the "Schloss Jagdstein," announces that he has killed the Archduke in a duel caused by his unrequited love, and then commits suicide by casting himself out of the high window for which the play is named.[3]

Although Munro made the protagonist of *Karl-Ludwig's Window* slightly older than the Prince of *The Death Trap* there is a similarity between these two militaristic playlets: finding a way out of an insoluble difficulty by committing a stiffly honorable suicide. Indeed, this Balkan setting, military background, and reverence for royalty would have been more suitable material for Munro's short stories, where they would not have seemed quite so ludicrous.

Both of these playlets may charitably be set down as mistakes of Munro's youth; apparently they were written as exercises, tentatively, before he determined to become a professional writer. Certainly their conception is very young, almost callow. About the only thing they indicate of the older Munro's writings is their mordant, rather nihilistic point of view.

II *A Comedy of Manners*

Obviously, Munro was well aware of the financial rewards of a stage success. In his exertions as an all-around writer he seems to have made a determined effort to write a play that would satisfy the needs and demands of the London commercial theater. Apparently he was on the point of having a commercially acceptable comedy produced just as the war broke out; very possibly he could have earned a considerable amount of money from it in the sweepstakes of the theater. It is a pity, in a way, that he did not attain sudden wealth; it is amusing to speculate on just what Munro would have done with a suddenly acquired small fortune —something highly original and imaginative, no doubt.

For this, his full-length play, a comedy, Munro reverted to the material and the backgrounds he knew from experience and to the sort of people with whom he was really familiar, those in the little world of upper-middle-class England. This play complements and amplifies, therefore, the gallery of characters Munro created in his short stories: the idlers, cynics, and nitwits of this little upper world. Munro titled his play *The Watched Pot* and, judging from internal evidence, he had begun composing it as far back as his St. Petersburg years.

Undoubtedly he knew all about the pitfalls confronting a new playwright in the risky world of the West End theater; and, with his natural prudence, he avoided any speculative production. In this raffish milieu he did not lower *his* standards of stringent personal behavior, but insisted upon conducting his theatrical enterprises with other gentlemen like himself. Munro seems to have been particularly fond of the Haymarket Theatre, which assisted the Establishment in its stately performance of the prescribed rites of the London season. The Haymarket somehow imparted to its patrons an ineffable air of refinement and of being "out of the top drawer." This theater appears in *The Unbearable Bassington* under the name of the "Straw Exchange Theatre"; Munro wrote that it was filled with "a distinguished and distinguishable people who made their appearance as a matter of course at a First Night in the height of the Season. Pit and gallery were already packed with a throng, tense, expectant and alert, that waited for the rise of the curtain. . . . Stalls and boxes filled slowly and hesitatingly with a crowd whose component units seemed for the most part to recognize the probability that they were quite as interesting as any play they were likely to see."[4]

Since the Haymarket Theatre obviously represented all that was right and preferable in London society, Munro submitted his play to Frederick Harrison, a Cambridge man who held the lease of the Haymarket Theatre, and Cyril Maude, Harrison's partner and star actor. Harrison and Maude were always alert for new scripts which would allow them to present themselves favorably to their public. In those days the great British actors had their own theaters and supervised the production of the plays in them, from the crucial matter of financing down to the smallest details of scenery and costumes.

Harrison and Maude were obviously gentlemen, a species unusual enough in the London theatrical world to attract Munro; they were also literate enough to appreciate Munro's authentic if snobbish characters and settings. Cyril Maude was, like Munro, the son of an officer in the Indian Army. He could trace his ancestry back to the twelfth century, to one of the assassins of St. Thomas à Becket, and so qualified for Munro's standards of breeding and for his reverence of medievalism. Maude, eight years older than Munro, was an "old boy" from Charterhouse, where he may possibly have known Munro's brother Charlie, a fact that illustrates the interlocking directorate nature of the enterprises of the British upper classes.

Munro's play was given a serious reading at the Haymarket offices, both as the contribution of a socially acceptable person and as a potential vehicle for an actor's tour de force. Maude severed relations with Harrison about 1906 and started his own independent venture in the Playhouse Theatre with his actress wife, Winifred Emery. Munro chose to go with Maude, and after a short time, the actor started to collaborate with Munro on the preparation of *The Watched Pot* for eventual production.

Maude wrote in a letter to Munro's sister, which Ethel reprinted as a sort of introduction to the published version of *The Watched Pot*, that

> The circumstances of our writing "The Watched Pot" were: Mr. Frederick Harrison was very interested in your brother's original "Watched Pot" but found it unsuitable for the stage, and brought Saki and myself together in the hope that our joint efforts would make it

suitable. My share was shortening it, giving it incident, and generally shaping it for stage purposes. Saki used to write more as a novelist than a playwright.

He and I used to have many friendly quarrels, as he was so full of witty remarks that it was a cruel business discarding some of his *bon mots*. We always used to terminate such quarrels by agreeing to use his axed witticisms in our next play. . . . Shortly before the war Saki at last gave in on the question of plot, and we had practically completed an entirely new story, still retaining the characters which he loved so dearly and which were so typical of his brain.[5]

The setting of the play is the country house of Hortensia Bavvel in Somerset, the sort of background that Munro intimately knew and understood, and which he reproduced with such authority. The "watched pot" of the play's title is Trevor Bavvel, a young man of twenty-six who, under the terms of his deceased father's will, is to inherit a sizable fortune and the property called "Briony Manor" when he decides to marry. But Trevor seems to be very choosy about the girl who is to be his mate; and, in the interval between Trevor's father's death and Trevor's marriage, Hortensia, Trevor's mother, is given temporary control of the estate by the terms of the dead father's will. Hortensia is a meddling and domineering old woman whose managerial proclivities have been reinforced by the terms of this will. Relatives, friends, and even servants naturally desire to see the more broad-minded and humane administration of Briony Manor which would prevail under young Trevor. His getting married in order that he may inherit the estate is therefore a most desirable and pressing matter to all hands.

The Watched Pot deals, as might be expected, with the machinations of a group of young females visiting at Briony to snare this extremely eligible bachelor. They are Agatha Clifford, a clumsy outdoor type; Clare Hennessey, equivocally nubile; Sybil Bomont, who is continually extricating herself from the attentions of an unwanted admirer who wanders inanely into the story; and Mrs. Peter Vulpy, a social-climbing grass widow. There are also Ludovic Bavvel, Hortensia's middle-aged brother, who takes an interest in politics and plans to campaign for a seat in Parliament, and René St. Gall, a useless, amoral, but amusing young fellow drawn very much in the tradition of Reginald.

After three acts of flippant dialogue and consistent frivolity, highlighted by an improvised dance and party in Hortensia's absence, which naturally Hortensia walks in on, the plot of the play is resolved by Trevor's disclosure that he has been married secretly for some time to Clare. It seems that the young couple could not reveal their marriage because Clare's great-aunt was conducting a feud with Hortensia, and the great-aunt of course forbade Clare to have anything to do with the Bavvel household.

But Clare's great-aunt fortuitously dies, allowing the resolution of the play's problems: the passing of the suzerainty of Briony Manor to Trevor, Ludovic's acceptance as a Parliamentary candidate, René's employment as Ludovic's secretary, and the retention of the disgruntled servants. Best of all, there is now a cease-fire among the young women who had battled to become Mrs. Trevor Bavvel. The play suffers from the stiffness of the theatrical conventions of the 1914 London stage, beginning with the unreasonable terms of a scarcely credible will, and ending with a still more improbable device: the resolution of the enmity between two families by a death, *à la* Montagues and Capulets.

The Watched Pot, for all its typical Munrovian attempts at originality in writing about the didoes of a group of young people, may very definitely be catalogued as a comedy of manners. It meets all of this medium's standards of lightness, flippancy, cynicism, and artificiality. The play acknowledges, without apology, the existence of a leisured class; and it dissects without apology their peccadilloes, affairs, and high-born attitudes.

Like the *Reginald* stories, the play's flavor and tone may best be inferred by quotations from it:

Says Ludovic:

"My late brother Edward, Hortensia's husband, who was not given to making original observations if he could find others ready-made to his hand, used to declare that marriage was a lottery. Like most popular sayings, that simile breaks down on application. In a lottery there are prizes and blanks; no one who knew her would think of describing Hortensia as either a prize or a blank." [6]

The character Sybil Bomont observes:

"A husband with asthma has all the advantages of a captive golf ball; you always know pretty well where to put your hand on him when you want him. . . . A woman who takes her husband about with her everywhere is like a cat that goes on playing with a mouse long after she's killed it." [7]

And René St. Gall, the empty-headed fop:

"I'm walking around practically naked. This suit I've got on was paid for last month, so you may judge how old it is." [8]

And:

"I know a lady up in Warwickshire who runs a rabbit farm. She has musical boxes set up over the hutches . . . they play the wedding march from 'Lohengrin' at decent intervals." [9]

Trevor Bavvel speculates:

"Think of the millions of nice women there are in the world, and then the fact that one can only marry one of them. . . . It's like choosing which puppies you're going to keep out of a large litter; you can never be sure that you haven't drowned the wrong ones." [10]

From Mrs. Vulpy:

"Nothing is more discouraging than to have a man say that you've ruined his life, and then to find out that you haven't even given him after-dinner insomnia." [11]

And from Clare Hennessey:

"One can afford to be neglected by one's own husband; it's when other people's husbands neglect one that one begins to talk of matrimonial disillusion." [12]

And the unbearably bossy character of Hortensia, which is really the point around which the play turns, is dissected in some detail. Her brother-in-law Ludovic says of her:

"She engaged and dismissed gardeners, decided which of the under-gamekeepers might marry and how much gooseberry jam should be made in a given year, regulated the speed at which perambulators might be driven through the village street and the number of candles which might be lighted in church on dark afternoons without suspicion of Popery. . . . Her gubernatorial energies overflowed the limits of the estate and parish, and she became a sort of minor power in the moral and political life of the county. . . . She . . . exposed the hitherto unsuspected atheism of the nearest Dean and Chapter, and dismissed a page-boy for parting his hair in the middle." [13]

As he often did when he drew the portraits of fictional characters, Munro used a live model for his study of this horrible old lady. Ethel wrote: "The character of Hortensia Bavvel is from life, but the tyranny of her prototype was confined to her own family." [14]

If the collaboration with Cyril Maude on the tightening up of *The Watched Pot* had no tangible pecuniary reward, at least it imparted to Munro some knowledge of what sort of material was wanted in the odd world of the theater; and he gave a good deal of thought to the special techniques of playwriting. Munro wrote thus of an author of a play: "Above all he had remembered that in the laws of stage proportions it is permissible and generally desirable that the part should be greater than the whole; hence he had been careful to give the leading lady such a clear and commanding lead over the other characters of the play that it was impossible for any of them ever to get on level terms with her. The action of the piece was now and then delayed thereby, but the duration of its run would be materially prolonged." [15] Munro apprehended this one great fact of the star system, which prevailed in the theater then as now; and, in spite of it, perhaps, he was a fairly frequent visitor to the inner sancta of actor-managers. He saw here the undressed, workaday side of the theater's evening glamor; the experience enabled him to write in *The Unbearable Bassington* of "great shroud-like dust covers being swathed over the ornamental gilt-work." [16]

Although Munro contested with Cyril Maude with a certain amount of contumacy over the axing of some of his dialogue, he surrendered at last to Maude's special knowledge of the practical theater. Munro's approach here, like his approach to all his other literary work, was that of a professional. By writing stage dialogue that was both witty and meaningful for a thoroughly sophisticated audience, Munro once again proved his literary flexibility. Sir John Squire called *The Watched Pot* the "most considerable of his promising dramatic efforts," and wrote that Munro's stage characters

> are consistent not with life, but with themselves and the queer world of his conception; and he contrives, even if he is realistic only in this limited way, to throw certain traits into a high light, and to express some . . . which are seldom expressed . . . there is a great deal of

unaccustomed candour in it. Where it differs from the Slavonic plays in which people naïvely bare their souls is not in any extra remoteness from daily life but in an occasional surprising contact with it. We can conceive of Tchekov, in his gloomier moments, as writing a play like *The Watched Pot* in which a household of women should all be trying to marry a placid young man with a gorgon of a mother, and all continually confessing to each other, egging each other on, scratching each other, or impudently maligning each other. Is "Saki" any more lacking in reality because he makes his dialogue witty, or because he shows cook, butler and housemaids as having a sweepstakes on the event in the servants' hall? And half his jokes depend for their force upon their exaggeration of truth. . . . "Saki" had all Wilde's cleverness at the substitution of a word in a stock saying or the inversion of a familiar proverb, and was an adept at contradicting our favourite clichés of word or thought, or strangely adapting them to unsuitable contexts. Yet though many of his sentences might be mistaken for Wilde's none of his pages could be attributed to another man.[17]

Munro could not refrain from introducing an irrelevant note on contemporary politics into a play that nominally concerned itself with husband-hunting women at a "county" mansion. A few of Munro's quips on the subject of British politics of that day are lifted from the third act of *The Watched Pot* and incorporated into the political discussion at Serena Golackly's card party in *The Unbearable Bassington.* This preoccupation with British politics runs like a highly visible thread through all of Munro's literary work; he really ought to have gone into politics himself, where with his lambent intelligence he could not have failed so dismally as most of the stuffed shirts who were helping to mismanage the civilized world into war.

Munro was unimpressed by marriage and the supposed happiness it brought into otherwise unfulfilled lives. He had one of his characters in his playlet *Karl-Ludwig's Window,* the Gräfin, utter these words about her son: "He said he should never marry any one he loved, so it didn't matter whom I married him to."[18] In many places in Munro's short stories and novels this disenchanted attitude toward marriage is unconcealed; but, if anything he wrote is concerned with the arranged, crassly pecuniary, sourly comic and unromantic aspects of marriage, *The Watched Pot* best qualifies as Munro's study of the institution. To him, marriage was not sacred beyond any fundamental criticism of it; but he was also in the tradition of his modish predecessors in the comedy of manners—Wycherley, Congreve, Sheridan, Wilde—in treating this institution with disrespect and cynicism.

The outbreak of World War I postponed the staging of Munro's play; and, by one of those ironies abundant in his work and in his life, he did not live to see a three-dimensional projection of "the characters he loved so dearly." After Munro's death, however, *The Watched Pot* was produced in several theaters of varying degrees of professionalism. This play, which now has the nostalgic charm of an authentic period piece, was staged at Cambridge in November, 1924, by the Amateur Dramatic Club, and again at the Arts Theatre in London in August, 1943, when it was part of a "festival of English comedy." *The Watched Pot* was chosen for production in this play cycle as being representative of the Edwardian comedy of manners.

In America, the Harvard Dramatic Club staged *The Watched Pot* in the spring of 1933; and, on what is now known as Off Broadway, an organization called On Stage produced it at the Cherry Lane Theatre in New York in the autumn of 1947. This version of *The Watched Pot* was reviewed favorably in the *New York Times* by Brooks Atkinson, who wrote wonderingly that the records showed that *The Watched Pot* had never been produced in New York before, and that the neglect of the play had been rather strange, considering the many plays of lesser worth that had been inflicted upon the playgoing public. Running for several months, *The Watched Pot* achieved a modest success in this New York production.

There is sufficient evidence in *The Watched Pot* to surmise that Munro, had he survived the war, would have been one of the great writers of English comedies in the 1920's, on the level of Somerset Maugham, Noel Coward, and Frederick Lonsdale.

CHAPTER 9

The Journalist as Jack-of-All-Trades

MUNRO remained a pragmatic journalist all of his writing life. Although the writing of short stories was his literary mainstay, enabling him to venture from time to time into the fields of novel writing, speculative playwriting, and political reporting, he was always ready to attempt journalistic odd jobs if they were acceptable to him. He had a commendably realistic attitude toward his journalistic work, but it had to measure up to his standards; Rothay Reynolds wrote that Munro "had to earn his living. . . . When a friend once suggested a profitable field for his writings, he dismissed the idea by saying that he was not interested in the public for which it was proposed that he should write."[1]

Munro never attempted to hide the fact that he practiced writing for a living: professionalism in writing was unquestionably his métier. It may have been an unseemly and somehow grubby manner of existence for one who was a sort of laureate of the idle elegance of the British upper world, but then Munro was never blessed with a private income of a size which enabled him to move in any other capacity except that of an observer through this world. Furthermore, Munro could never, by his independent and determined nature, have been a sponger or hanger-on, though he wrote authoritatively enough of this sort of parasite. He had, if not ambition, a self-discipline and an acceptance of hard work. The anomaly of Munro's social position, this having to work in the sweaty world of Fleet Street while he mixed with the snob world, was yet another irony in the career of a superb ironist.

I *Journalistic Odd Jobs for the* Bystander

As early as 1910 Munro was placing his rather specialized journalistic output with the *Bystander*, where Vivian Carter was a most understanding editor. Carter published a good deal of

Munro's work which strove for a degree of originality that it was dangerous to inflict on the readers of a glossy society magazine. Munro's first journalistic appearance in the *Bystander*, for instance, was not particularly apposite. In the issue of December 7, 1910, he wrote the captions for six pen-and-ink caricatures of current London theatrical celebrities. The innocent *Bystander* reader who read the captions beneath the drawings of such stage notables as Zena Dare, Sir Herbert Beerbohm Tree, and Lewis Waller in expectation of learning some new gossip about them must have been disappointed, if not actually baffled. Munro dragged in allusions to obscure personages of medieval history, to heraldry, to Russian geography, and to the insides of whales. This piece is overlaid with a whimsy and fantasy so *outré* that it has no relation whatever to the already zany world of the theater. It was Munro's first and last attempt at gossip paragraphing.

The series that Munro contributed to the magazine a year and a half later, featuring two of his specialties—current politics and disenchanted social comment—was more representative of the "Saki" tradition. During the summer of 1912 the *Bystander* published a series of "Heart-to-Heart Talks" which the magazine prefaced with the note: "We have no other authority than that of our contributor that the conversations between the persons in question have actually taken place—Editor." Each of Munro's articles fills one page of the magazine, about a thousand words; and they are subtitled with the names of current celebrities who allegedly conducted these imaginary dialogues.

Dialogue No. 1, subtitled "M. Nijinski and the Master of Elibank" (who was then the Chief Whip of the Liberal party), treats of Nijinski's supposed awareness of the machinery of British politics, and of the Master of Elibank's hitherto suppressed desire to write and stage an original ballet on the theme of the Day of Judgment. Attributing these fancies to his improbably juxtaposed principals allowed Munro to comment on such diverse idiocies then currently newsworthy as American ancestor worship, British opposition to social reforms, and the divisive effects upon England and Ireland of religious agitation in Ulster.[2]

The second "conversation piece" appeared in the *Bystander* two weeks later, subtitled "Mr. Bernard Shaw and Baron Marschall von Bieberstein." Von Bieberstein, the ambassador of Imperial Germany to the Court of St. James's, was of considerable interest to the *Bystander's* swank readership; but the piece deals exclusively with a satirical view of the archsatirist Shaw. As Munro presented him, Shaw was made to monopolize the entire conversation. Munro made Shaw believe that posterity would ungratefully rate him as a "chattering, posing, after-dinner-talkative individual" and that it would "attribute all my plays to Arthur Balfour." But it was really Shaw's socialism and his dilettante counseling of revolution that annoyed Munro and caused him to turn his considerable verbal weaponry upon Shaw whenever he was given the opportunity. In this instance, Munro allowed von Bieberstein to utter only one single word; the rest of the conversation is devoted to Munro's unflattering conception of Shaw.[3]

The final piece of this brief series, entitled "Mr. Hammerstein and Dom Manoel," permits Munro to show off his knowledge of Russian grand opera. The "Mr. Hammerstein" of the subtitle was an American impresario who wanted to interject another opera house into London's musical monopoly, and Dom Manoel was the recently deposed king of Portugal. Hammerstein, according to Munro, expected to fill his projected opera house by permitting audiences to wear the costumes of whatever opera was being staged. Hammerstein speculates: "Just imagine what the house would be like on a *Carmen* night, the mantillas and combs and roses in the hair, the toreador costumes and Spanish uniforms. How the audience would love themselves, and what crowds would gather outside to see them come in. What *éclat,* what advertisement, what receipts." [4]

In all three of these "Heart-to-Heart Talks" Munro made allusions and references so topical that they are almost incomprehensible to the modern reader, but his next venture into journalism for the *Bystander* was unequivocally political. That October, he regaled the Tory readers of the magazine with a book review of a totally imaginary autobiography by Lloyd George. "More About Him," Munro titled his tract, "The Fifth Volume of the Life of Mr. Lloyd George. Reviewed for 'the Bystander' of 1919." Munro's supposed book review was written in the form of extracts from Lloyd George's supposed diary: "Drove past Buckingham Palace. Shall I confess that I cast on the dingy pile the same envious eye that Charles Martel may have cast on the residence of the then Sovereigns of France? Vanity! And yet. . . . Cannot help thinking how well it would sound: David, by the acquiescence of God, of Wales and Little Britain King." In another diary excerpt, Munro presented his conception of Lloyd George through what he had him write: "Guy Fawkes Day. Usual heavy crop of arrests and prosecutions for unseemly choice of individual pilloried as Guy . . . during my triumphal drive through London, some fervent admirers endeavoured to indicate how cheap and abundant food had become under my administration by throwing eggs and tomatoes and portions of fish. . . ." [5]

Munro was apt, because of his detestation of Lloyd George, to abandon his objectivity and his sense of fair play. Seemingly, Lloyd George personified for Munro all those forces bound on abolishing the old ruling order with its many prerogatives and raising to the top of the British social scale those classes which were traditionally subservient and culturally untutored. Lloyd George himself was a most combative and bitter political opponent, and it was this quality of political effectiveness that made Munro consider him the most dangerous of those who advocated the overturn of the old order in Britain. Moreover, Lloyd George, besides his use of intemperate language, a failing which Munro never failed to seize upon, was obviously not a gentleman either by birth or by upbringing; this was enough for Munro to damn him. Lloyd George typified the thrusting commoner who dared invade the fountainhead of British politics at Westminster, that erstwhile preserve of gentlemen who, regardless of their party affiliations, were wellborn, moneyed, and leisured.

In 1913 Munro attempted to repeat the success of the *Westminster Alice* a dozen years earlier by collaborating with a cartoonist, one "Pat," whose identity has been lost in the musty files. Munro furnished the letterpress for this "Pat"-"Saki" collaboration: his contribution took the form of doggerel captions for "Pat's" crude cartoons. A comparison of "Pat's" work with Munro's own attempts at cartooning and sketching—efforts liberally sprinkled throughout the first edition of his sister's biography—establishes that they had at least one thing in common: they were both amateurs at drawing. "Pat" seems to have had something of Munro's enthusiasm for animals and birds because he introduced them into almost all of his pictures, but his representations of galloping and capering horses are stiffer and less lifelike than the horses Munro himself drew. In any event, "Pat" was certainly no F. Carruthers Gould, nor had he Gould's Daumierian gift of capturing on his penpoint the absurdities of current politics.

The first of these "Pat"-"Saki" efforts appeared in the *Bystander* of March 12, 1913. It was titled "The Metamorphoses of Lobelia Tabb, Suffragette," and to the accompaniment of twenty-four lines of Munro's doggerel such as

> A suffragette Lobelia was
> She early left this life because
> (She had the rottenest of luck)
> She too sincerely hunger-struck.

"Pat" drew the suffragette reincarnated as a wasp, a dog, an ape, and an English public school boy. The Conservative bias against the suffragette movement is very obvious in this two-page collaboration, in which "Pat" introduced likenesses, drawn most unflatteringly, of some of the leading Liberal politicians.

The second (and last) of these joint creations to appear in the *Bystander* was published on April 2, 1913. It was labeled "The Toothless Lion—A Fable of Diplomacy," and in its message it is very like the plea for British universal military service which Munro amplified in *When William Came.* Great Britain was drawn as the lion which was granted the divine boon of having no teeth, of being "delivered from the pain and inconvenience of cutting teeth in the days of its youth." When the British lion wanted to join its friends, the French Fighting Cock and the Russian Steppe-Eagle in their alliance against the German Wild Boar and the Austro-Hungarian Danube Eagle, the Lion asked "Shall I roar and lash my tail?" The Steppe-Eagle replied: "If you like . . . but remember that everyone knows you are without teeth." [6]

The "Pat"-"Saki" collaboration was carried over into the London daily press. During April and May of 1913, the "Pat"-"Saki" team sold four of their "creations" to the *Daily Express* which even then, before it had come under the control of Lord Beaverbrook, was a fiercely Conservative organ. The collaborations were now based on old English ballads and nursery rhymes, and they were even more politically partisan than the two *Bystander* pieces. Prime Minister Asquith, a Liberal, was drawn as a fat fool; Lloyd George, as a coward; Sir John Seely, the Secretary of State for War, as a complacent dupe; and Redmond, the leader of the Irish Nationalists, as a hunting dog who ran enthusiastically with the Liberal party.

Far from repeating the success of the *Westminster Alice* collaboration, the "Pat"-"Saki" series, like the *Not So Stories* of 1903, was dead and forgotten almost as soon as it was published.

II *Seemingly, a Firmly Jelled Routine*

In his last civilian years Munro had settled into a systematic way of life that can only be called a routine of dinner parties, theatergoing, and club-frequenting in town; but he also evinced a most uncharacteristic interest in the affairs of his country cottage on the Surrey Hills, for Munro was definitely an undomesticated type. Indeed, this defect or perhaps gap in his character had a strong influence on his writings. His repugnance for domesticity and the settled life appears all through his essay "Clovis on The Alleged Romance of Business." [7] A passage in this sketch shows very clearly his contempt of the nine-to-six routine and his dread of ever having to earn his living in the unutterable dreariness of some office: ". . . The business man [who] married early and worked late, and lived, thousands and thousands of him in little villas outside big towns. He is buried by the thousands in Kensal Green and other large cemeteries; any romance that was in him was buried prematurely in shop and warehouse and office. Whenever I feel in the least tempted to be business-like or methodical or even decently industrious I go to Kensal Green and look at the graves of those who died in business." [8]

And Munro was fortunate, from his viewpoint, in being able to avoid this particular form of regimentation throughout his life. His refusal to "marry and settle down" was an integral part of his revulsion against domesticity and the constricted life of a bowler-hatted office worker. His minority opinion of domesticity and marriage runs through his fiction. Two excerpts from his writings very candidly state his lack of regard for the settled-down life:

He was a bachelor of the type that is called confirmed and which might better be labelled consecrated; from his early youth onward to his present age he had never had the faintest flickering intention of marriage. Children and animals he adored, women and plants he accounted somewhat of a nuisance. A world without women and roses and asparagus would, he admitted, be robbed of much of its charm, but with all their charm these things were tiresome and thorny and capricious, always wanting to climb or creep in places where they were not wanted, and resolutely drooping and fading away when they were desired to flourish.[9]

. . . A man who stood outside the marriage-tie as a philosophic and satirical onlooker, the attitude of a Manx cat towards a cat that has got its tail jammed in a door.[10]

Some latter-day sidelights on this aspect of Munro's life are given by J. W. Lambert: "His sister once, after his death, let drop —and appeared to regret having let drop—a remark to the effect that there was at one time the possibility of a match between him and a Lady Rosalind Northcote, but that it fell through because he had not enough money. . . . Dornford Yates suggests that he may have put the idea of marriage from him because after their father's death he assumed full responsibility for his difficult, not to say impossible, sister.[11]

Whatever the reason for his estrangement from the supposed joys and fulfillment of matrimony, Munro in his writings never had a kind word for the institution; but he seems to have had some concern for keeping his family contacts alive. Wrote Ethel, in a reference to these last prewar years: "Charlie was at this time with his wife and child in Dublin, where he was Governor of Mountjoy Prison, having left the Burma Police service; though stronger than Hector, the climate rather told on him. Hector and I spent Christmas with them one year and next summer we were all together again on the Donegal coast at Innishowen." [12]

Munro seems to have left an impression of strength of character, of individuality, and of charm on the people who knew him at this time. Lord Charnwood wrote of "the real Hector, whom his friends knew, tender-hearted, caring for things lovely and of good report, caring for them passionately, and every inch a man." [13] And Ethel quoted from an anonymous friend: "The elusive charm of the man-in-himself—this charm, being the perfume of personality, was even more subtly, strongly felt in his conversation than in anything he ever wrote. We who loved him as the kindliest of companions who was utterly incapable of boring a fellow-creature —man or dog or woman or cat or child of any age you like—always felt the keen sense of honour and strength of purpose and stark simplicity which were his essential qualities."[14]

Another glimpse of Munro at that time was captured by Thomas Anstey Guthrie: "I met Hector Munro again at an evening party on the 12th of December [1913] when he gave an extremely funny imitation of Sarah Bernhardt reciting a French version of 'The Walrus and the Carpenter'."[15] This anecdote is revelatory of the wide extent of Munro's elegance and sophistication, and of the glittering world he frequented. Yet his sister Ethel's biography gives one the mental picture of Munro commuting like a property-loving homebody from Mortimer Street to his cottage in Surrey, so stodgily bourgeois, so distressingly suburban.

The most detailed and informative picture of Munro's work habits and living routine during this last London period is to be found in the memoir by Rothay Reynolds in *The Toys of Peace*:

> He had a lodging in Mortimer Street and lived exceedingly simply. It was his custom to pass the morning in a dressing-gown writing. His writing pad was usually propped up with a book to make it slant and he wrote slowly in a very clear hand, rarely erasing a word or making a correction. His air and the movement of his hand gave one the impression that he was drawing and not writing. He almost always lunched at a Lyons bread-shop,[16] partly because it was economical and partly because, as he said, he got exactly the sort of luncheon he liked. He cared nothing for money. . . . He would share his last sovereign with a friend, and nothing pleased him better than to entertain his friends at dinner in a club or restaurant.[17]

Munro's home in town at 97 Mortimer Street has escaped the attention of the London County Council, the organization that has placed many of its blue and white commemorative plaques on other London houses which have sheltered British authors. It does seem prodigal, though, to ignore the workroom of one of England's greatest satirists.

Indicative of Munro's involvement with the London journalistic world was his presence at the dinner which the *Bystander*, in a graceful gesture from the magazine's directors to the people who provided the copy, the drawings and the photographs for its weekly appearance gave to its contributors on January 19, 1912, at the Trocadero Restaurant in London. The *Bystander* supplemented its flashlight photograph of the party (showing Munro seated in the rear) with a little report headed "The 'Bystander' Dines Out." It is an interesting insight into the methods Munro used to keep in with the movers and shakers of his own rather narrow field of London journalism.

And Munro kept one foot in the camp of the critics and the literati. As a professional writer, he was more or less compelled to stay on good terms with these influential people, however much he might deride the affectations he found in their grandiloquent company. An example of this type of necessary literary kowtowing was his attendance, on June 20, 1914, of a tea party given by John Lane in his little business establishment in Albany. The party's purpose was to provide a reception for the Canadian writer Stephen Leacock, who was then being promoted as a budding humorist. Munro rubbed elbows at this reception with many of the famous literary names then adorning English letters, and another amusing mental picture is thereby conjured up—Munro balancing his teacup in the shoehorn tightness of the mass of writers, critics, and social and political dignitaries packed into John Lane's small business quarters, exchanging insincerities of a literary nature with one another, and of Munro missing no gaucherie of speech or behavior that might be transmuted through his sensibilities into material for his fiction.

Munro was now forty-three years old, an age when a comfortable way of life and the good regard of one's peers held much more attraction for him than they had when he was twenty-three and starting out on a writing career. Surely he would never again experience a rough and violent life, on the order of his adventures as a policeman in Burma, or his exploits and hazardous enterprises as a foreign correspondent, when he witnessed violence, uprisings, bloodshed, and mass murder. These experiences were now in his distant past, their memory remote and half-forgotten. If there is an echo of such stirring times in his later fiction, it is set down in a rather detached mood of recollection, like the remembrance of an insistent drumbeat in some long ago parade. Munro was settled, secure, and of very good repute. If he were not careful, he would presently be regarded as a pillar of the London literary community.

III *The Last Assignment*

In the frenetic world of Fleet Street Munro could be relied upon to submit his accurately written copy by a prescribed deadline. Because of his dependability and his professional approach to his journalistic work, Munro was a jewel, if not beyond price, which in his case seems to have been quite modest, to harassed editors. Undoubtedly, this dependability was considered when he was chosen to cover the 1914 spring session of Parliament for yet another London weekly, the *Outlook*.

This magazine was about as Conservative politically as Munro himself; indeed, he himself may have had the happy inspiration of writing about Parliamentary sessions for it. The *Outlook* was owned by a Conservative Member of Parliament, Walter Guiness, who as Lord Moyne thirty years after this period, was assassinated in Egypt by Israeli nationalists. The *Outlook* was written to Munro's standards of literate good taste, but was one-sided; once again, Munro's work appeared in an organ which was congenial both politically and intellectually. The *Outlook*'s fierce partisanship, compounded of its advocacy of the union of Ireland and England, its reverence for tradition, and its opposition to reform gave Munro a most welcome platform. An example of the *Outlook*'s faithful Toryism was its discovery of the "Marconi scandal."

In the summer of 1912 the *Outlook* had been the first periodical to publish the rumors about supposed corruption in the highest levels of the Liberal party because the Post Office had awarded a government contract to the Marconi Company for the eventual transmission of long distance telegrams by means of radio to all parts of the British Empire. Many were the magazine's innuendoes about the honesty of members of the Liberal government's cabinet: here was partisanship after Munro's own heart.

In obtaining this assignment from the *Outlook* Munro had achieved the pinnacle of his reporting on the actions of parliaments. He had written, through his previous journalist years, on the happenings within the Austro-Hungarian Reichsrath, the Bulgarian Sobranje, the first Russian Duma, and the Chamber of Deputies in Paris; now at last he could observe the actions of the representatives in the "Mother of Parliaments" in London. To receive payment in coin for the excitement of witnessing and reporting Parliament's actions was almost a superfluity.

The British Parliament was opened for its new session on February 10, 1914, with all the pageantry of a long national history. The weather was unseasonably warm; the day, sunny and bright. While the crowds around the House of Commons awaited the arrival of royalty, they were entertained with music from the military bands of the Household troops. It was a pleasing scene: the flocks of pigeons wheeled skyward whenever the bells of St. Margaret's Church or the booming of Big Ben shivered the clear air, and the scarlet uniforms of the troops made vivid streaks against the good-natured crowds. Like the fine weather, Britain's power and prestige were a sparkling pleasure to behold.

Upon the *Outlook*'s nomination of Munro as its Parliamentary reporter, he was issued the necessary press pass by Parliament's sergeant-at-arms. After identifying himself to the satisfaction of the guardian policeman at the Parliamentary gate at New Palace Yard, through which all the journalists had to enter the Houses of Parliament, he entered the special journalist's door, mounted a narrow stairway, and entered the cramped press gallery fourteen feet above the Speaker's chair in the House of Commons.

The House of Commons had many customs and traditions peculiar to itself, many of them inherited from the *faineant* and aristocratic makeup of its membership in earlier times. It had unconventional hours of session, from 2:45 P.M. until 11:00 P.M. on Mondays through Thursdays, and from noon until 5:00 P.M. on Fridays, to allow for the joys of the upper-class weekend. Many members wore their high silk hats while in attendance. Government and opposition members were not allowed to approach one another across the dividing lines on the floor, which represented the length of a sword. Members used a courtly method of locution when speaking of one another.

Munro naturally knew of these hoary customs; after all, he was of the Establishment; and the House of Commons from its inception, until very recent times, had been a sort of preserve for the well bred and the well-to-do. Munro himself had the usual well-born attitude of proprietorship toward the House. And there was always the comforting thought that, even in these increasingly egalitarian times, the House had a preponderance of gentlemen.

Munro's political enemy, the Liberal party, retained the administration of the British government by its coalition with the Irish Nationalist party—Ireland still sent representatives to Westminster in those days—and with the support of the then minor Labour party. The Conservative, Munro's party, simply could not muster enough votes in the House of Commons to overrule the Liberal party's coalition legislation on a redistribution of Britain's wealth, a strengthening of the political power of the working class, or Home Rule of Ireland from a Dublin Parliament. The Liberal coalition passed its innovative legislation with an air of helping the underdog against unreasonable opposition, but Munro seemed to think that the Liberals always acted from motives of political profit, with a hateful self-righteousness, while all they really succeeded in doing was to tear down everything that centuries of subservience and tradition had accreted.

This conflict between Munro's Tory attitudes and the stream of precedent-breaking legislation passed by Parliament makes his series of *Outlook* reports lively and involved, for his talents for satire and well-bred invective would never have been so evident in these articles had his own party been in power. And the Parliamentary session of 1914 was remarkable for its turbulence and rancor and portentousness. In its constant eventfulness it was a reporter's dream, and Munro himself finally called it "this momentous and critical session." There was a continuing agitation for the betterment of the condition of the British working class, spurred by the threat of impending industrial unrest on a vast scale, especially on the railways. The issue of Home Rule for Ireland was most rancorous and divisive, and there was a distinct possibility of a civil war over it which would rend the British Isles like nothing since the time of Oliver Cromwell. Over the other critical issue with which the 1914 Parliament had to contend shrilled the continuing advocacy of women's right to vote. The front-line fighters in this struggle, the suffragettes, gave constant demonstrations of their militancy by breaking plate-glass windows, by various forms of arson, by physical attacks upon their male opponents, and by other spectacular methods of advertising their cause, which continually echoed through the houses of Parliament. For Munro, it was a stirring thing to be an onlooker at the creation of such raw history.

In the fervor of Munro's Parliamentary causeries of the next twenty-four weeks may be seen the deep animosity between the magnificoes of Britain's two great political parties, the animosity which had sprung up during the preceding few years. Some Liberal hostesses did not invite Conservatives to attend their dinner parties, and some Conservative hostesses did not invite Liberals—the "war to the knife and fork." And Munro's unkind regard toward an Englishman who has since been beatified by history, Sir Winston Churchill, is quite typical of Munro's partisan approach. Munro had many opportunities to observe Churchill in action in the House—Churchill then served the Liberal government as First Lord of the Admiralty—and could not forgive and forget Churchill's abandonment of the Conservative party a decade earlier. In one of Munro's dispatches, to which he gave the generic heading "Potted Parliament," he wrote of Churchill: "It could never be said that Mr. Winston Churchill is not in a position to be a shrewd judge of the gentleman caste; the outsider proverbially sees most of the game." [18] Munro was also quite unkind to the Labour party's Parliamentary spokesman, Ramsay MacDonald. Munro wrote that MacDonald was "lion-maned and mouse-prudent," but there is some truth mixed in with the bitter humor of this capsule description.

But it was the Liberal politician who personified the social and economic reforms of the preceding decade, David Lloyd George, who was the most infuriating figure to the Tories, and thus, to Munro. Lloyd George had the knack of getting under their collective skin; and they considered him a cad, a low-born thruster, and a bounder. Munro fully subscribed to this view of Lloyd George, who was now the Chancellor of the Exchequer in the Liberal government. Munro wrote in the *Outlook*: "There should surely be set up a commemorative tableau of Mr. Lloyd George lost in ecstatic contemplation of an Insurance Act and several Budgets. . . . The exuberant financial projects of Mr. Lloyd George are scattered and strewn in wanton profusion over the Treasury bench and called a Budget. . . . Lloyd George squatted on the Treasury bench with the detached air of a water-newt that has produced a million eggs and refuses to be discomfited because seven hundred thousand of them are addled." [19]

The explosive situation in Northern Ireland was a recurring theme in Munro's Parliamentary dispatches. The determination of the Roman Catholics in the south of Ireland to be governed by their own semi-independent parliament, which would sit in Dublin, was complemented by the determination of the Ulster Protestants to remain an integral part of Great Britain. The Liberal party was kept in power in London by its coalition with the Irish Nationalist party, which had the Liberal party's promise to legislate Home Rule for Ireland. In this situation, all of Munro's sophisticated superiority to formal religion was abandoned. It was a time for choosing sides, and Munro wrote his "Potted Parliament" dispatches as a Protestant, a Unionist, and a member of the Establishment.

When certain high-ranking officers of the British army were allowed to signify their refusal to participate in any military move to suppress the illegal army of Protestants in Northern Ireland, the Secretary of State for War, Sir John Seely, was forced to resign because of his weakness in handling this dissidence. Thereupon Prime Minister Herbert Asquith took over the control of the war office in addition to his other duties. Munro commented: "Now at least the Prime Minister knows what the War Minister is doing." [20]

In obbligato to these momentous issues of social change and religious controversy shrilled the voices of the suffragettes demanding the right of women to vote; and, as on the other great issues of the day, Munro took a firmly reactionary stand. He was so absorbed in these domestic crises that he lost his usual perception and failed to predict the grave international crisis which erupted late that July. The crisis burst upon him as it had upon men even more informed than he. He wrote from Parliament on July 27: "Black Mondays have been plentiful during the course of the present session, but none of them have been quite so black in outlook and retrospect as the one that ushered in the workdays of this doleful week. One had the curious spectacle of party passions roused to a fierce pitch over the course of domestic events, and damped down by the consciousness of a threatening outside danger." And Munro also wrote of "the overhanging gloom of the international situation." [21]

Munro's final Parliamentary dispatch, printed in its entirety by his sister in her biography, imparts the tense atmosphere of the House of Commons on August 3, 1914, when the Foreign Secretary, Sir Edward Grey, delivered his ultimatum to Imperial Germany. Munro—with his natural bellicosity, his deep sense of honor, his Tory nationalism—was, of course, all for war. Not for him was the sad, apprehensive sentiment of Sir Edward's celebrated remark, made during the last hours of England's ultimatum, about the lights going out all over Europe.

At the declaration of war Munro immediately abandoned whatever writing commitments he had made. His considerable knowledge of the nations on the Continent, his skepticism and his pervasive sophistication might have been expected to lead him into a projection of the war's beastliness and its ultimate toppling of that social system for which he had such regard. But, instead, Munro was as jubilant over the war's outbreak as London's poorest and most naïve. Munro typified the intelligent, educated European who went enthusiastically to war in August, 1914, expecting to find in that holocaust a kind of personal and national redemption.

CHAPTER 10

The Gentleman Ranker

UPON the outbreak of war Munro conducted himself with uncharacteristic excitement, and he frantically attempted to find a military unit which would accept him. There is an eyewitness account of his rather feverish behavior at this time, for Rothay Reynolds wrote:

> That night we dined at a chop-house in the Strand with two friends. On our way Munro insisted on walking at a tremendous pace, and at dinner, when he ordered cheese and the waiter asked whether he wanted butter, he said peremptorily: "Cheese, not butter; there's a war on." A day or two later he was condemning himself for the slackness of the years in London and hiring a horse to take exercise, to which he was little addicted, in the Park. He was determined to fight. . . . In the first weeks of the war there seemed little chance of his being able to become a soldier. "And I have always looked forward to the romance of a European war," he said.[1]

The "romance" of war for which Munro longed came from a dream world of chivalry and glamor, of cavalry charges, hand-to-hand combat, pennant-flying expeditions, and unfailingly chivalrous conduct by all the combatants. It was the common dream of millions in August, 1914; but these conditions of warfare had vanished with Napoleon. The Industrial Revolution had now taken over the waging of war; the slaughter was conducted impersonally by huge machines in the service of vast conscript armies; and the combatants seldom saw their enemy. Nevertheless, Munro and millions like him went into combat eagerly.

I *An Overage Recruit*

Munro finally succeeded in joining as an enlisted man a newly formed volunteer unit of cavalry under the command of John Norton-Griffiths, a Conservative Member of Parliament—a unit which after some truly comic Blimp-ery was allowed to call itself the 2nd King Edward's Horse. The Master of Elibank, now Lord Murray, was another of the founders of the 2nd King Edward's Horse; and, as Munro had been almost beastly to him in print, it is rather strange that Munro was accepted into this particular unit, but apparently personal feelings were considered to be unimportant in August, 1914.

Rothay Reynolds commented further on Munro's behavior in that momentous month: " . . . he was supremely happy. He put on a trooper's uniform with the exaltation of a novice assuming the religious habit." [2] One reason for the exaltation may have been that Munro had joined a cavalry unit and had visions of charging the enemy on the back of a galloping horse, a fairly prevalent idea in 1914 of what warfare was going to be like. He could claim and prove a good knowledge of horses and riding, and he could cite his experience in a mounted unit of the Burma Police twenty years before; but, when he had succeeded at last in joining the cavalry, he was unable to measure up to its demanding routine. The plunging, whinnying steeds were a heavy responsibility; and their care was compounded by the added handicap of primitive living conditions for the soldiers. Munro admitted the rigors of these early military conditions in a letter to his sister, written from another unit seven months later: "The work is hard some days but it is not incessant like it was in the K. E. H." [3] And Rothay Reynolds wrote of the inevitable outcome: "But after a few months he found that he was not strong enough for life in a cavalry regiment and he arranged to exchange into the 22nd Royal Fusiliers." [4]

The 22nd (Service) Battalion Royal Fusiliers was an infantry outfit, also entirely volunteer, which was partially formed from young Londoners who had signed up to join Kitchener's "New Army." Munro was not the only would-be cavalryman to be severed from and left behind by the 2nd King Edward's Horse when it moved on to Buckinghamshire. Several hundred colonials languishing at the White City in September, 1914 were allowed to amalgamate with the Londoners to form the 22nd Battalion Royal Fusiliers. Munro was assigned to "A" Company as a colonial (apparently he claimed a Burmese connection). He had finally found a secure footing in the British army.

Actually, he should never have been permitted to join a combat unit. His background of writing and his extensive experience in Eastern Europe—now enemy territory with restive and unhappy populations—should have shouted out that Munro ought to be utilized in military intelligence. It is conceivable that, had Munro been sent to Russia in 1916, he would have done more, with his firsthand knowledge of the country, to avert the eventual seizure of the Russian revolution by the Bolsheviks than some of his British literary contemporaries who tried to keep Russia in the war, writers like Hugh Walpole and Somerset Maugham. At the very least Munro should have been persuaded into taking a commission; at least twice he refused the offer of a commission on the grounds that he had not enough martial knowledge to be an officer. Considering the thousands of incompetent officers then to be found in the British army, it was a ridiculous reason.

The student soldiers of the 22nd Battalion Royal Fusiliers got their basic training within the grounds of one of London's commandeered amusement parks, the White City, surrounded by the tunnel of love, the Ferris wheel, and the scenic railway. The incongruity of these surroundings could not have been lost on the sweating recruits; and, as for Munro, it was just another of life's ironies, although one of exceptional comicality.

A highlight of these early training days was the battalion's march, through Bayswater and along Oxford Street to the Tower of London, to draw rifles. The battalion returned from the Tower by way of Piccadilly, proudly bearing real weapons and enjoying the approbation of crowds still demonstrative in the first flush of patriotism. Munro may be visualized on this occasion as looking very stern and purposeful as he swung past the haughty establishments of St. James's and the fashionable streets of Mayfair, where so many of his fictional creations had languidly strolled, effete and foppish.

For Munro, it must have been a salutary and very educational experience to mix with a group of men whose backgrounds were mostly working class; their company undoubtedly gave him insights into the attitudes and folkways of the British masses which would never have been vouchsafed to him in the rigid peacetime separation of the classes. Munro was so obviously a gentleman, so authentically to the manor born, that it must have taken a lot of mutual adjustment to fit him in compatibly to "A" Company, 22nd Royal Fusiliers. There were, of course, many "gentleman rankers" in the British army then, particularly in the first year of the war, when all good men wanted to get in a lick at the German enemy before the war should come to a quick end. All the same, it must occasionally have been irritating to the bulk of the others to listen to Munro's diction, so "la-de-da" in the upper class way.

There must have been times, too, when Munro was bored with the society of the Feebles, the Bullcalfs, the Mouldies—this Munro whose deep sophistication could take the form of imitating at a dinner party Sarah Bernhardt reciting "The Walrus and the Carpenter" in French. But he, who had been an intimate of the anointed, the washed, and the elect was now the familiar of crude and unlettered men to whom he would have had nothing to say in peacetime.

Munro seems to have been a competent recruit, although he did not excel in the polishings and rather mindless drillings of a soldier's drab barracks routine. The indifference might have been due to his comparatively advanced years, when a man should have the tin soldier complex in its proper perspective; but, at any rate, he did not excel at drill, and actually seemed to do fatigue duties in preference to it. Munro was not at all regimental, or a stickler for form; he seemed to consider the routine of camp life rather silly, a nuisance to be tolerated until the day when the battalion should go into combat.

In October, 1914, the battalion moved to Horsham in Sussex and in March, 1915, it went to a newly built camp in nearby Roffey. The battalion then went north in the summer of 1915 to Clipstone Camp near Nottingham, finally moving south again for a rigorous period of outdoor living on Salisbury Plain at Tidworth. In November, 1915, it became apparent that the 22nd Royal Fusiliers was about ready to enter combat. Munro wrote to his sister from Tidworth on November 7th: "After long months of preparation and waiting we are at last on the eve of departure and there is a good prospect of our getting away this week. It seems almost too good to be true that I am going to take an active part in a big European war. I fear that it will be in France, not the Balkans, but there is no knowing where one may find oneself before the war is over; anyhow, I shall keep up my study of the Servian language. . . . I expect at first we shall be billetted in some French town." [5] On November 16, 1915, after being reviewed by Queen Mary, the battalion left England for France via Folkstone and Boulogne; and Munro was on the way to fulfilling an obsessive dream—to fight in the war.

II *The Writer as Combat Infantryman*

The 22nd Battalion Royal Fusiliers reached France intact on November 17, 1915, at a strength of thirty officers and nine hundred and ninety-two men. The next day they entrained from Boulogne for Steenbeque, where they stayed in billets for a few days; they then marched through Thiennes, St. Venant, and Bethune until, on November 26, they reached a comparatively quiet stretch of the front at Annequin. With curiosity, the 22nd eyed a haggard unit just relieved from duty in the trenches; but the 22nd itself soon began to send working parties to quick tours of trench duty to acclimate them to the rifle fire, the shellbursts, and the mud. Munro described the setting as being compounded of: "The rattle and rumble of transport, the constant coming and going of bodies of troops, the incessant rattle of musketry and deafening explosions of artillery, the night-long flare and flicker of star-shells." [6]

After this preliminary taste of trench life Munro was sent back of the line for instruction at an N.C.O.'s school, rejoining the battalion at Festhubert in the middle of January, 1916, where the battalion was living and fighting under extremely waterlogged conditions. By February 3, the battalion had moved to Givenchy, and Munro wrote home about an incident there:

> We are holding a rather hot part of the line and I must say that I have enjoyed it better than any we have been in. There is not much dugout accommodation so I have made my bed (consisting of overcoat and waterproof sheet) on the fire-step of the parapet; on Sunday night, while I was on my round looking up the sentries, a bomb came into the trench, riddled the overcoat and sheet and slightly wounded a man sleeping on the other side of the trench. I assumed that no 2 bombs would fall exactly on the same spot, so remade the bed and had a good sleep.[7]

Munro never described the beastliness of the war in his articles or in his letters home from France. Yet the Gethsemane of trench warfare must have been more of a psychological burden for him than for the stolid, unimaginative types around him. The spurting of blood, the screams of the wounded and dying, the pervasive odor of decomposing flesh, the universal filth, the animality of life in the trenches dispelled, one would think, any illusions Munro had in 1914 about the reality of twentieth-century warfare, an illusion implicit in what he said to Rothay Reynolds in August, 1914 about the romance of war.

Munro did, however, write of the incredibly foul conditions in which the soldiers had to endure the fighting:

> In narrow-dug support-trenches, when thaw and heavy rains have come suddenly atop of a frost, when everything is pitch-dark around you, and you can only stumble about and feel your way against streaming mud walls, when you have to go down on hands and knees in several inches of soup-like mud to creep into a dug-out, when you stand deep in mud, lean against mud, grasp mud-slimed objects with mud-caked fingers, wink away mud from your eyes, and shake it out of your ears, bite muddy biscuits with muddy teeth, then at last you are in a position to understand thoroughly what it feels like to wallow.[8]

For Munro continued to write for publication even at the front. He turned out three compositions while rotated from duty in the trenches: "For the Duration of the War" (which has a footnote in its collected form "written at the Front"); "The Square Egg," subtitled "A Badger's-Eye View of the War Mud in the Trenches"; and "Birds on the Western Front." All of these pieces have the authority of participation in their descriptions of the front line and of the battered rest area back of it. It was the reappearance of the oldtime reportorial ability to write well under extreme pressure. Rothay Reynolds commented on Munro's combat writing: " 'When peace comes,' wrote an officer of the 22nd Royal Fusiliers . . . 'Saki will give us the most wonderful of all the books about the war'." [9]

Again, Munro was offered a commission and again he refused it, nor would he allow anyone to alleviate the conditions under which he served in the trenches; for, as Rothay Reynolds reported:

> I was told by a man of his company that one day a General was conducted along the trenches by the Colonel commanding the regiment and recognized Munro, whom he had met at dinner-parties in London. "What on earth are you doing here?" he asked, and said that he had a job to be done at the rear which would be the very thing for him. Munro excused himself from accepting it. Another opportunity of less

arduous work was offered him. Men who could speak German were ordered to report: interpreters were wanted to deal with prisoners. Munro reported, but urged that it had taken him two years to get out to the front and that he desired to remain there.[10]

From March to May, 1916, the battalion served in the area of Souchez; but it was sent toward the end of May on a hurry call to the developing battle of Vimy Ridge, where it fought a heavy engagement in its first over-the-top action, around the Tallus de Zouaves. Munro's demeanor at such perilous times may be divined from this passage: "Once, having occasion to throw myself down with some abruptness on my face, I found myself nearly on top of a brood of young larks. Two of them had already been hit by something, and were in rather a battered condition, but the survivors seemed as tranquil and comfortable as the average nestling." [11]

In early summer Munro came back to England on leave. Ethel wrote:

> In June 1916 Hector came back on short leave: Charlie and I hurried to London and all three put up at the Richelieu (now Dean) Hotel. It was a breathless time, with friends and relatives coming to see him, theatres, the Academy and shopping. He showed signs of wear and tear, but was in great spirits. . . .
>
> This delightful time in town passed with lightning swiftness, and the day came for us to see him off at Victoria, Charlie and I and a friend, never thinking it was the last time we should see him.[12]

Munro returned to France in time to participate in one of the 22nd Royal Fusiliers' biggest battles at Delville Wood, a part of the great Somme offensive. A friend of Munro's, W. R. Spikesman, who had known him in civilian life, was also a member of the 22nd Royal Fusiliers; and he has given an eyewitness account of Munro's behavior and demeanor at Delville Wood:

> Delville Wood in August, 1916 is vivid in my memory because of the terrible gunfire experienced, and the undaunted bravery and courage of "Saki." Just imagine a wood, the trees battered to splintered stumps, trenches about two feet deep, no definite trench line, troops from many battalions in isolated knots having during the attack become disintegrated, looking for leaders, ready to attach themselves to

any officer as long as they had some one to command them, a terrific fire from enemy batteries (I remember one shell which fell to my right killing 16 men) and so many dead.

Hector on this occasion even surprised me, who had always tried to emulate some one worth while; he stood and gave commands to frightened men, in such a cool, fine manner that I saw many backs stiffen, and he was responsible for the organization of a strong section, giving them a definite "front" to face, and a reassuring word of advice.[13]

And Munro himself wrote his own description of Delville Wood in a piece for the *Westminster Gazette*:

At the corner of a stricken wood (which has had a name made for it in history, but shall be nameless here), at a moment when lyddite and shrapnel and machine-gun fire swept and raked and bespattered that devoted spot as though the artillery of an entire Division had suddenly concentrated on it, a wee hen-chaffinch flitted wistfully to and fro, amid splintered and falling branches that had never a green bough left on them. The wounded lying there, if any of them noticed the small bird, may well have wondered why anything having wings and no pressing reason for remaining should have chosen to stay in such a place. There was a battered orchard alongside the stricken wood. . . . The only other bird I ever saw there was a magpie, flying low over the wreckage of fallen tree-limbs; "one for sorrow," says the old superstition. There was sorrow enough in that wood.[14]

The battalion was relieved from Delville Wood on August 4, and for the next month or so served in the trenches around Hebuterne. In September Munro was promoted to Lance-Sergeant, a not very impressive step considering his demonstrated leadership and his advanced years. Later that autumn he became seriously ill when the battalion moved into the wet and muddy trenches around Acheux Wood. W. R. Spikesman wrote of this: "About October, 1916, malaria, a fever that had attacked him in India when a boy, sent Hector to the M.O., who asked no questions but immediately sent him back to the Base."[15] Ethel described his chafing impatience during this hospitalization: "He wrote to Charlie from hospital, full of impatience at being laid up, and feeling very lonely among strangers. 'I keep thinking of the boys all the time: when one is sharing dangers they don't seem big, but when one is in safety and the others in the front line all sorts of catastrophes seem possible and probable'."[16]

News of a coming British attack upon Beaumont Hamel in which Munro's battalion would participate filtered back to the hospital at Rouen. Munro, with all the determination of his stubborn soul, resolved to be in the thick of it. There is something of the tragic inevitability of this decision in the lines which Munro composed, not too long before, for his short story "For the Duration of the War":

> There is a sadness in each Dawn,
> A sadness that you cannot rede
> The joyous Day brings in its train
> The Feast, the Loved One, and the Steed.
>
> Ah, there shall come a Dawn at last
> That brings no life-stir to your ken,
> A long, cold Dawn without a Day,
> And ye shall rede its sadness then.[17]

W. R. Spikesman wrote of this last gesture of Munro's:

> . . . although the attack on Beaumont Hamel was a sure thing, the date was uncertain, but Hector heard it at the Base and I saw him again about the 11th of November. He looked a very sick man and should have been in bed, but I knew his thoughts and the reason for his being fit. We were in position by 3 A.M. on 13th November, 1916, left of Beaumont Hamel in front of "Pendant Copse" and the Quadrilateral, and remained there until the early morning of the 14th November, when we left our front line to "flank out" on the left of our advanced line.
>
> It was a very dark winter morning, but after much excitement we were hailed by voices and a figure rose to the top of the trenches in front of us and shouting greetings to the Company commander . . . engaged him in conversation. A number of the fellows sank down on the ground to rest, and Hector sought a shallow crater, with the lip as a back-rest. I heard him shout, "Put that bloody cigarette out," and heard the snip of a rifle shot. Then an immediate command to get into the trenches. It was sometime later, about an hour, when a fellow came to me and said, "So they got your friend." [18]

Munro had been killed by a shot through the head.

CHAPTER 11

Conclusion

ANALYZING Munro's work is a singularly difficult and unrewarding job; for, as Christopher Morley noted, ". . . there are fewer writers less profitable to write *about.*" Munro's rather acid wit, his singular fantasies, his highly unusual viewpoint somehow succeed in making critical dissections of these qualities seem clumsy and imperceptive. No commentator on his work has been really successful in attempting to isolate and precisely define individual aspects of the "Saki" manner, though these critics to a man can glibly express their appreciation. It would seem that Munro was truly *sui generis.* J. C. Squire stated the problem more subtly: ". . . the precise flavour of 'Saki' is as easy to recognize and as impossible to define as that of a good Claret or Hock." [2] And there is much truth in these observations. Munro is a most elusive subject both as man and writer, and he poses a problem for his commentators because these two aspects have seldom been so inextricably mixed as in Munro's fiction. Hugh Walpole wrote of this "Saki" rareness: ". . . the first most obvious reason for this survival lies in this uniqueness. . . . When we consider the work of any contemporary writer that must be one of the most important questions that we can ask of him; is he unique? is he doing something that nobody else has done before him?" [3]

Undoubtedly Munro broke new literary ground in his fiction; his quiet, disenchanted observations, inserted so suavely into his stories, on the human animal's foibles and follies, his mockery of human values, beliefs, institutions, his masterly use of the macabre, his great and constant wit, his genuine cosmopolitanism, and even his habitual use of surprise endings are some of the ingredients which were blended into the truly idiosyncratic works of "Saki." This work was fresh, if more than a little unsettling; and it was completely underived, owing nothing to any predecessor.

One can, however, eliminate Munro as a reforming influence on his contemporaries. Two of the best-known of Munro's reform-minded contemporaries, H. G. Wells and Bernard Shaw, attacked the established order to varying degrees. Wells, writing mostly about the working and the lower-middle classes, was deeply critical of the economic and social systems of that time. Shaw, the parlor revolutionary, preached abolition of every class distinction and privilege which was dear to Munro. If these two writers read Munro—and there is nothing to suggest that they ever did—they would have been repelled by his cynical disbelief in the perfectibility of man and by his resistance to any form of social improvement. Undoubtedly, they would have dismissed him as just another insensitive Tory snob, amusing perhaps, and a damnably capable writer, but as one with such antediluvian social views that his work could not possibly be of any value.

Rather, it was to more worldly contemporaries that Munro appealed, to writers like A. A. Milne, the elegant Maurice Baring, J. C. Squire, Ford Madox Ford, the young Hugh Walpole, and to writers of the P. G. Wodehouse stripe generally—men who have admitted Munro's influence. The "Saki" style and subject matter appeared quite often in the prewar fiction of this kind of uninvolved writer. And Munro was an example and a model to a good many aspiring writers who were then attempting to break into the glossy magazines and the best of the London newspapers. All the same, Munro's influence must have been subdued—one might say unobtrusive. He was not in the least interested in the literary coteries or cliques of his time; most certainly, he was not a "lit'ry" man.

Munro's real accomplishment was to recognize the potential of the story material in the denizens and in the trappings of the upper classes. To him almost alone goes the credit of discovering and working this rich vein—the shallowness of the paladins who ordered his era and his world. Munro stands alone as *the* satirist of the grossnesses of Edwardian society; one cannot think of a better qualified Petronius in this narrow but fruitful field. This, then, is his contribution to English literature.

In Munro's cool, detached manner—his lack of involvement with his characters—can be seen his qualifications, had he lived, for being one of the most penetrating writers of the 1920's. The 1920's, a time whose vast disillusionment he had anticipated ten or fifteen years before, would have been a perfect setting for him.

Munro was more than just clear-eyed and unsentimental: he observed his characters with the complete detachment of a pathologist regarding specimens on a dissecting table, and with this approach he would have fitted in beautifully in the postwar world.

During this decade Munro's influence, acknowledged or tacit, is much greater; many of the descriptions of the heightened insanity of the 1920's owe much to the Munro manner. Munro's fiction, wrote George Dangerfield, displayed "a singular anticipation of the young man of 1925." [4] Munro would have been a "natural" for the disillusioned 1920's, a more trenchant Noel Coward, a wider-ranging Scott Fitzgerald, a more literate Michael Arlen.

How Munro would have fitted into the hungry 1930's or the World War II era is not easy to judge. He would have had a terrible time adjusting to the far-reaching changes in England's economic system and to the vast upheavals in that social order which he had always upheld as the best possible order for stupid humankind. His audience, which widened immeasurably with the revival of his books in the 1920's would not have found him very amusing had he been revived in the 1930's. Paradoxically, his talent is not suited to a time of hunger and disintegration; but whatever he would have written would have been presented with his customary polish, originality and distinction.

Notes and References

Chapter One

1. Ethel M. Munro, "Biography of Saki," in *The Square Egg* by H. H. Munro (New York, 1929). This sketch of twenty-five thousand words was composed after Munro's death. It is the prime source of biographical material about him. It is disjointed, with strange emphases and hardly any analysis of Munro's writing, and it is curiously reticent —"all I have cared to tell of Hector's life" (p. 102).

2. Nikolaus Pevesner, *The Buildings of England-North Devon* (Harmondsworth, Middlesex, 1952), pp. 135–37.

3. The contemporary British critic J. W. Lambert wrote in his Introduction to *The Bodley Head Saki* (London, 1963): "This unhappy woman grew to be so fiercely possessive, first of her brother, then of his memory, that having written her own fragmentary memoir she refused access to, and subsequently destroyed, all Saki's papers."

4. Graham Greene, *The Lost Childhood* (London, 1951), pp. 74–76. Graham Greene wrote about Munro in the essay lugubriously entitled "The Burden of Childhood." This is perhaps the most eloquent pleading of the case that the corrosive effects of the "deprived" Broadgate childhood profoundly influenced Munro's work. Yet Munro's childhood plight is not unique: Thackeray and Kipling were also brought to England from the East in their childhood and reared by strangers.

5. E. Munro, "Biography of Saki," *The Square Egg* (New York, 1929), p. 19.

6. *Ibid.*, p. 4.

7. Letter to *The Spectator*, June 13, 1952, p. 780.

8. E. Munro, "Biography of Saki," p. 22.

9. "O. B. G." in *The Bystander*, December 15, 1909, p. 584.

10. John Sergeaunt, *A History of Bedford School* (London, 1925), pp. 143–48.

11. J. W. Lambert, Introduction to *The Bodley Head Saki* (London, 1963), p. 9.

12. E. Munro, "Biography of Saki," p. 24.

13. *Ibid.*, p. 27.

14. *Ibid.*, p. 27.
15. *Loc. cit.*
16. E. Munro, "Biography of Saki," p. 29.
17. H. W. Nevinson, Introduction to *Beasts and Super-Beasts,* collected edition (New York, 1928), p. viii.
18. "Potted Parliament," *The Outlook,* May 9, 1914, p. 626.
19. *The Square Egg and Other Sketches with Three Plays,* collected edition (New York, 1929), pp. 137–38.
20. *The Unbearable Bassington,* collected edition (New York, 1928), p. 185.
21. E. Munro, "Biography of Saki," pp. 32–47.
22. Saki, *Filantropen och den Lyckliga Katten,* trans. by John Karlzen (Stockholm, 1948), pp. 147–90.
23. E. Munro, "Biography of Saki," pp. 31 and 47.

Chapter Two

1. *When William Came* (New York, 1929), p. 230.
2. *Ibid.*, pp. 219–20.
3. In a letter published in the April 14, 1900, edition of *The Athenaeum,* p. 466, Munro wrote on this point: "Among the yeomen and peasantry of the west of England . . . there still lingers a genuine and practical belief in witches and white and black magic, presumably a relic of a much earlier cult . . ."
4. E. Munro, "Biography of Saki," pp. 48–49.
5. *Ibid.*, p. 51.
6. *The Rise of the Russian Empire* (London, 1900), p. vii.
7. *Ibid.*, p. 53.
8. *Ibid.*, p. 177.
9. *Ibid.*, p. 62.
10. *Ibid.*, p. 81.
11. *Ibid.*, p. 96.
12. *Ibid.*, p. 124.
13. *Ibid.*, p. 131.
14. *Ibid.*, p. 201.
15. *Ibid.*, p. 216.
16. *Ibid.*, p. 219.
17. *Ibid.*, pp. 37–40.
18. Lord Charnwood, Introduction to *When William Came,* p. x.
19. Edward Garnett. Review of *The Rise of the Russian Empire, The Bookman* (London), August, 1900, pp. 155–56.
20. Archibald Carney Coolidge. Review of *The Rise of the Russian Empire, The American Historical Review* (New York), October, 1901, pp. 138–40.
21. E. Munro, "Biography of Saki," p. 51.

Chapter Three

1. J. W. Lambert, Introduction to *The Bodley Head Saki*, pp. 26–27.
2. E. Munro, "Biography of Saki," p. 49.
3. A. A. Milne, Introduction to *The Chronicles of Clovis* (New York, 1927), pp. ix–x.
4. J. A. Spender, Introduction to *The Westminster Alice* (New York, 1929), pp. vii–viii.
5. Munro used this *nom de plume* for the rest of his life, but his books were published with the name "H. H. Munro" in brackets under "Saki" on their title pages. It is difficult to see the point of writing under a pseudonym in these circumstances, except perhaps that Munro did not care to use his own name because it had been preempted by another contemporaneous novelist. Another Hector Munro was being published about that time, one of his novels being *Mrs. Elmsley*.
6. *The Westminster Alice* (New York, 1929), pp. 27–28.
7. J. A. Spender, Introduction to *The Westminster Alice*, p. xi.
8. *Ibid.*, p. xii.
9. *The Westminster Alice*, p. 98.
10. *Ibid.*, p. 105.
11. J. A. Spender, Introduction to *The Westminster Alice*, p. viii.
12. Oddly enough *The Westminster Alice* received a fervid welcome in America when it was published in the Collected Edition in 1929. American readers seemed to disregard any ignorance of the figures of a quaint, long-vanished British political scene. The American publishers in their trade paper, *The Viking Log*, of November 18, 1929, apologized to the booksellers for being out of stock on *The Westminster Alice:* "We frankly warned the dealers not to overstock this book, since we consider it the least salable of the eight volumes, good as it is. However, the public took matters into its own hands and re-orders came so fast and heavy that we were swamped." Here belatedly was additional proof that Gould and Munro had succeeded in capturing the charm of the original *Alice* books, the common heritage of the English-speaking world.
13. E. Munro, "Biography of Saki," p. 54.
14. J. W. Lambert, Introduction to *The Bodley Head Saki*, p. 34.
15. E. Munro, "Biography of Saki," p. 61.
16. Maurice Baring, *The Puppet Show of Memory* (Boston, 1922), p. 332.
17. The Duchess may have been patterned upon Lady St Helier, whose salon of literary and political figures Munro frequented at this period.

18. *Reginald and Reginald in Russia* (New York, 1928), p. 4.
19. *Ibid.*, pp. 10–11.
20. *Ibid.*, pp. 15–16.
21. *Ibid.*, pp. 20–21.
22. *Ibid.*, p. 28.
23. *Ibid.*, p. 35.
24. *Ibid.*, p. 40.
25. *Ibid.*, p. 44.
26. *Ibid.*, p. 66.
27. *Ibid.* pp. 52–53.
28. John Gore, *Edwardian Scrapbook* (London, 1951), pp. 128–29.
29. *Ibid.*, p. 129.
30. Hugh Walpole, Introduction to *Reginald and Reginald in Russia*, pp. viii–ix.
31. *Reginald and Reginald in Russia*, pp. 21–22.

Chapter Four

1. E. Munro, "Biography of Saki," p. 54.
2. Anonymous, *Morning Post* (London, November, 1916).
3. H. W. Nevinson wrote in his Introduction to *Beasts and Super-Beasts* that Munro was well suited to correspond for the *Morning Post*. "He was endowed," Nevinson observed of Munro, "with just the right touch of 'educated scorn' which has always distinguished that superior paper. Like his paper, 'Saki' was suspicious of all enthusiasm, especially of all Liberal enthusiasm."
4. E. Munro, "Biography of Saki," p. 54.
5. *The Toys of Peace* (New York, 1928), pp. 221–22.
6. *Morning Post* (London, January 28, 1903), p. 7.
7. E. Munro, "Biography of Saki," p. 54.
8. *The Toys of Peace*, pp. 222–23.
9. E. Munro, "Biography of Saki," p. 54.
10. *Ibid.*, pp. 56–59.
11. *Morning Post* (London, May 7, 1903), p. 5.
12. *Ibid.* (June 15, 1903), p. 7.
13. *Ibid.* (March 1, 1904), p. 5.
14. *Ibid.* (April 5, 1904), p. 5.
15. *Ibid.* (May 3, 1904), p. 5.
16. *Morning Post* (London, May 5, 1904), p. 8.
17. E. Munro, "Biography of Saki," p. 64.
18. *Morning Post* (London, January 25, 1905), p. 5.
19. E. Munro, "Biography of Saki," pp. 61–63.
20. *Ibid.*, pp. 63–64.
21. H. W. Nevinson, *More Changes More Chances* (New York, 1925), p. 105.

22. *Morning Post* (London, November 11, 1905), p. 7.
23. *Ibid.* (May 11, 1906), p. 4.
24. E. Munro, "Biography of Saki," p. 68.
25. *Morning Post* (London, November 14, 1907), p. 5.
26. A. A. Milne, Introduction to *The Chronicles of Clovis,* p. xi.
27. *The Unbearable Bassington,* pp. 107–8.
28. J. C. Squire, Introduction to *The Square Egg,* p. xi.

Chapter Five

1. Ethel Munro, "Biography of Saki," p. 68.
2. Rothay Reynolds, Memoir in *The Toys of Peace* (New York, 1928), p. xix.
3. *Reginald and Reginald in Russia,* p. 183.
4. E. Munro, "Biography of Saki," p. 69.
5. Rothay Reynolds, Memoir in *The Toys of Peace,* p. xx.
6. Francis Toye, *For What We Have Received* (New York, 1948), pp. 113–15.
7. *Beasts and Super-Beasts* (New York, 1928), p. 117.
8. Ben Travers, *Vale of Laughter* (London, 1957), pp. 47–68.
9. Rothay Reynolds, Memoir in *The Toys of Peace.*
10. E. Munro, "Biography of Saki," p. 49.
11. Sir John Squire, Introduction to *The Square Egg,* pp. xii–xiii.
12. E. Munro, "Biography of Saki," p. 87.
13. *The Chronicles of Clovis* (New York, 1927), pp. 39–44.
14. *The Toys of Peace,* pp. 184–86.
15. *Beasts and Super-Beasts,* pp. 112–14.
16. *When William Came* (New York, 1929), pp. 42–43.
17. H. W. Nevinson, Introduction to *Beasts and Super-Beasts,* p. vii.
18. *The Toys of Peace,* pp. 143–44.
19. *Ibid.,* pp. 19–22.
20. *The Chronicles of Clovis,* p. 145.
21. E. V. Knox, Introduction to *76 Short Stories* (London, 1956), p. 14.
22. *Beasts and Super-Beasts,* pp. 235–39.
23. *The Square Egg* (New York, 1929), p. 130.
24. *Reginald and Reginald in Russia,* p. 170.
25. *Beasts and Super-Beasts,* p. 151.
26. *The Chronicles of Clovis,* pp. 115–22.
27. *Reginald and Reginald in Russia,* p. 135.
28. *The Toys of Peace,* p. 137.
29. *The Chronicles of Clovis,* pp. 69–74.
30. Munro's stories were adapted for television by Gerald Savory, Hugh Leonard, and Edward Boyd.

31. Thomas Anstey Guthrie, *A Long Retrospect* (London, 1936), p. 332.

32. Sir John Squire, Introduction to *The Square Egg*, p. xii.

33. A. A. Milne, Introduction to *The Chronicles of Clovis*, pp. xi–xii.

34. *Beasts and Super-Beasts*, p. 74.

Chapter Six

1. Munro had previously used this theme of the misfit who upset the lives of the conventional people around him in the short story "Bertie's Christmas Eve." Munro wrote of Bertie: "At the age of eighteen Bertie had commenced that round of visits to our Colonial possessions, so seemly and desirable in the case of a Prince of the Blood, so suggestive of insincerity in a young man of the middle-class. He had gone to grow tea in Ceylon and fruit in British Columbia, and to help sheep to grow wool in Australia. At the age of twenty he had just returned from some similar errand in Canada."

2. E. Munro, "Biography of Saki," p. 76.

3. *The Unbearable Bassington*, p. 2.

4. *Ibid.*, p. 222.

5. Rothay Reynolds in his Memoir (pp. xviii–xix) tells of the extent to which Comus Bassington's nostalgia in West Africa was based on Munro's own sensations: "He once told me of the feeling of loneliness he experienced when he first arrived in Burmah [*sic*], using almost the same words in which he described Bassington's sense of isolation in the colony to which he was sent. That account of the young Englishman looking enviously at a native boy and girl, racing along in the joy of youth and companionship, is one of the rare instances of autobiography in Munro's works."

6. E. Munro, "Biography of Saki," p. 76.

7. Hugh Walpole, Introduction to *Reginald and Reginald in Russia*, p. ix.

8. *The Unbearable Bassington*, p. 187.

9. Indicative of the modern interest in this book by professional British writers is the passage written by James Agate in his *Ego 9* (London, 1948), p. 48: "March 17, 1946. Reply to an unknown correspondent, telling me that he is the original of Comus in Saki's *The Unbearable Bassington*. This gives me a real thrill. Munro's masterpiece is one of my favourite bed-books. *I never tire of it*. . . . I should like to meet [you] in the flesh. Will you lunch with me on any date you like to name at the Ivy Restaurant, 1:30. . . . In the meantime I start tonight re-reading the book for the seventh time."

10. Maurice Baring, Introduction to *The Unbearable Bassington* (New York, 1927), pp. ix–x.

11. Evelyn Waugh, Introduction to *The Unbearable Bassington* (London, 1947), pp. v–viii.
12. *The Unbearable Bassington,* p. 90.
13. *Ibid.,* p. 178.
14. *Ibid.,* p. 178.
15. *Ibid.,* pp. 93–94.
16. *Ibid.,* p. 94.
17. *Ibid.,* p. 30.

Chapter Seven

1. It is finely ironic that Guy du Maurier died in combat against an actual German army in France, like Munro himself.
2. *When William Came,* p. 159.
3. Ethel Munro wrote ("Biography of Saki," p. 76) that the character of Lady Eleanor had been drawn from that of "a well-known London Conservative hostess, for whom Hector had a great admiration."
4. Munro's club, the Cocoa Tree (now defunct), is mentioned in the book (p. 99) under the transparent disguise of "the Cockatrice Club."
5. *When William Came,* p. 191.
6. E. Munro, "Biography of Saki," p. 76.
7. *Ibid.,* p. 83.
8. *Ibid.,* p. 76.
9. Thomas Anstey Guthrie, *A Long Retrospect,* p. 339.
10. *When William Came,* pp. 132–33.
11. *Ibid.,* p. 36.
12. *Ibid.,* p. 156.
13. *Ibid.,* pp. 30–32.
14. *Ibid.,* p. 33.
15. *Ibid.,* pp. 148–50.
16. *Ibid.,* pp. 218–19.
17. *Ibid.,* p. 144.
18. *Ibid.,* pp. 137–38.
19. G. K. Chesterton, Introduction to *The Toys of Peace* (New York, 1928), p. xii.
20. *When William Came,* pp. 39–40.

Chapter Eight

1. E. Munro, "Biography of Saki," p. 29.
2. *Ibid.,* p. 35.
3. The dizzying view down from this window was an actual boyhood experience of Munro's. His sister described the incident, on the

Munro family's second wanderjahr on the Continent ("Biography of Saki," p. 26): "Prague was another delight, particularly Wallenstein's castle. . . . In one room high up, formerly a council chamber, we were shown the window from which obstreperous councillors were thrown; we leant out while my father hung on to us, to see the depth they had to fall. This is the one described in 'Karl-Ludwig's Window.'"

4. *The Unbearable Bassington,* p. 177.
5. *The Square Egg,* p. 162.
6. *Ibid.,* p. 166.
7. *Ibid.,* p. 178.
8. *Ibid.,* p. 188.
9. *Ibid.,* pp. 205–6.
10. *Ibid.,* p. 201.
11. *Ibid.,* p. 226.
12. *Ibid.,* p. 241.
13. *Ibid.,* pp. 167–68.
14. *Ibid.,* p. 162.
15. *The Unbearable Bassington,* p. 183.
16. *Ibid.,* p. 192.
17. Sir John Squire, Introduction to *The Square Egg,* pp. xiii–xv.
18. *The Square Egg,* p. 153.

Chapter Nine

1. Rothay Reynolds, "Memoir of H. H. Munro," in *The Toys of Peace,* p. xx.
2. The *Bystander,* July 17, 1912, p. 118.
3. *Ibid.,* July 31, 1912, p. 230.
4. *Ibid.,* August 14, 1912, p. 330.
5. *Ibid.,* October 2, 1912, p. 18.
6. *Ibid.,* April 2, 1913, p. 35.
7. In 1931 the advertising department of the *National Geographic Magazine* reprinted "Clovis on the Alleged Romance of Business" in pamphlet form, illustrated with photographs of Latakia, Zanzibar, Alkmaar, Smyrna, Kyoto, Rangoon and the lagoon of Kauehi, among other places. This pamphlet was obviously aimed at those malcontents in business who were forced to stay at home and vegetate.
8. *The Square Egg,* p. 136.
9. *When William Came,* pp. 68–69.
10. The *Bystander,* July 31, 1912, p. 230.
11. J. W. Lambert, Introduction to *The Bodley Head Saki,* p. 36.
12. E. Munro, "Biography of Saki," p. 75.
13. Lord Charnwood, Introduction to *When William Came,* p. ix.
14. E. Munro, "Biography of Saki," p. 78.

15. Thomas Anstey Guthrie, *A Long Retrospect*, p. 338.
16. The Lyons chain of cafeterias is the London equivalent of the New York Automats. One wonders what Munro, the gourmet who wrote so lovingly of plover's eggs and artichokes *vinaigre*, found to tempt his palate on the Lyons menu.
17. E. Munro, Memoir in *The Toys of Peace*, pp. xix–xx.
18. The *Outlook*, March 25, 1914.
19. *Ibid.*, May 16, 1914, p. 677.
20. *Ibid.*, April 4, 1914, p. 452.
21. *Ibid.*, August 1, 1914, pp. 134–35.

Chapter Ten

1. Rothay Reynolds, Memoir in *The Toys of Peace*, pp. xxi–xxii.
2. *Ibid.*, pp. xxi–xxv.
3. E. Munro, "Biography of Saki," p. 85.
4. Rothay Reynolds, Memoir in *The Toys of Peace*, p. xxv.
5. E. Munro, "Biography of Saki," p. 89.
6. *The Square Egg*, p. 117.
7. E. Munro, "Biography of Saki," p. 91.
8. *The Square Egg*, p. 105.
9. Rothay Reynolds, Memoir in *The Toys of Peace*, p. xv.
10. *Ibid.*, p. xxvi.
11. *The Square Egg*, p. 116.
12. E. Munro, "Biography of Saki," pp. 92–93.
13. *Ibid.*, pp. 100–101.
14. *The Square Egg*, pp. 116–17.
15. E. Munro, "Biography of Saki," p. 101.
16. *Ibid.*, pp. 93–94.
17. *The Toys of Peace*, p. 231.
18. E. Munro, "Biography of Saki," pp. 101–2.

Chapter Eleven

1. Christopher Morley, Introduction to *The Short Stories of Saki* (New York, 1930), p. v.
2. Sir John Squire, Introduction to *The Square Egg*, p. xi.
3. Hugh Walpole, Introduction to *Reginald and Reginald in Russia*, p. vii.
4. George Dangerfield, *The Strange Death of Liberal England* (New York, 1935), p. 433.

Selected Bibliography

PRIMARY SOURCES

The Rise of the Russian Empire. London: Grant Richards, 1900.

The Westminster Alice. London: *The Westminster Gazette,* 1902.

Reginald. London: Methuen, 1904.

Reginald in Russia. London: Methuen, 1910.

The Chronicles of Clovis. London: John Lane, The Bodley Head, 1911.

The Unbearable Bassington. London: John Lane, The Bodley Head, 1912.

When William Came. London: John Lane, The Bodley Head, 1913.

Beasts and Super-Beasts. London: John Lane, The Bodley Head, 1914.

The Toys of Peace (collected and published posthumously). London: John Lane, The Bodley Head, 1919.

The Square Egg and Other Sketches (collected and published posthumously). London: John Lane, The Bodley Head, 1924.

Articles and correspondence in the *Westminster Gazette,* the *Morning Post,* the *Daily Express,* the *Bystander* and the *Outlook,* all of London.

The Collected Edition:

The Chronicles of Clovis, with an introduction by A. A. Milne. New York: The Viking Press, 1927.

The Unbearable Bassington, with an introduction by Maurice Baring. New York: The Viking Press, 1927.

Beasts and Super-Beasts, with an introduction by H. W. Nevinson. New York: The Viking Press, 1928.

Reginald; and Reginald in Russia, with an introduction by Hugh Walpole. New York: The Viking Press, 1928.

The Toys of Peace, with an introduction by G. K. Chesterton, and a memoir by Rothay Reynolds. New York: The Viking Press, 1928.

The Square Egg and Other Sketches with Three Plays, with an introduction by Sir John Squire and a biography of Saki by Ethel M. Munro. New York: The Viking Press, 1929.

When William Came, with an introduction by Lord Charnwood. New York: The Viking Press, 1929.

The Westminster Alice, with an introduction by J. A. Spender. New York: The Viking Press, 1929.

SECONDARY SOURCES

ANDERSSON, INGVAR. Foreword. *Det Fyrkantiga Ägget och Andra Historier av Saki.* Translated into Swedish by John Karlzen. Stockholm: *Natur och Kultur,* 1947. Ingvar Andersson's foreword is interesting because it views Munro's work from a different vantage point, the world of Scandinavia. Andersson is most appreciative, although he seems to find Munro a rather introverted writer in these translations of twenty-three of his short stories.

Anonymous. "Saki," *New Statesman,* XXVII (July 24, 1926), 416. A review of three of Munro's books then emerging in the British collected edition (*Reginald, Beasts and Super-Beasts,* and *The Chronicles of Clovis*). Although it speaks admiringly of Munro's rare wit, it emphasizes his preoccupation with the cruel, the macabre, and the supernatural.

BARING, MAURICE. *The Puppet Show of Memory.* Boston: Little, Brown and Company, 1922. A fine, colorful picture of life in St. Petersburg during the period when Munro wrote from there. Baring succeeded Munro as the *Morning Post*'s St. Petersburg correspondent.

BRAILSFORD, H. N. *Macedonia: Its Races and Their Future.* London: Methuen and Company, 1906. Brailsford, representing the *Manchester Guardian,* went out from England to Macedonia in company with Munro. This book's text and many photographs show just how primitive were the people and places on which Munro had to report.

Burma. Police Department. *Report on the Police Administration of Burma.* Rangoon: 1895. Tabulates the incidence and type of crimes committed in Burma in 1894. Valuable for an understanding of Munro's policeman period. Brief mention of Munro's brother Charlie.

DANGERFIELD, GEORGE. *The Strange Death of Liberal England.* New York: Harrison Smith and Robert Haas, 1935. Excellent survey of British history from May, 1910, to August, 1914, a period of continual economic and political turmoil: the emasculation of the House of Lords, the rise of the suffragettes, critical labor unrest, and probable civil war in Ireland.

DONALDSON, FRANCES. *The Marconi Scandal.* New York: Harcourt, Brace & World, Inc., 1962. Shows how deep and bitter was the animosity between the Conservative and Liberal parties in 1913, a feeling reflected in Munro's articles from Parliament the following year.

DRAKE, ROBERT. "The Sauce for the Asparagus." *The Saturday Book No. 20*, London: The Macmillan Company, 1960. Discusses the dated, lost-world impression Munro's work makes on the modern reader.

DU MAURIER, GEORGE. *English Society*. New York: Harper & Brothers, 1897. In a series of a hundred and fifty pen-and-ink sketches Du Maurier brilliantly illustrated the milieu in which Munro lived through his young manhood.

EDES, E. M. and FRASIER, DUDLEY, eds. *The Age of Extravagance: An Edwardian Reader*. London: Weidenfeld and Nicholson, 1955. Aspects of high life in England in the first decade of this century as described by various authors. Munro is represented by a chapter from *The Unbearable Bassington*.

GORE, JOHN. *Edwardian Scrapbook*. London: Evan Brothers, Ltd., 1951. Devotes a chapter, "A Literary Prototype of the Age," to Munro.

GOULD, GERALD. "Saki," *New Statesman*, X (November 17, 1917) 159–60. Most appreciative review of Munro's work, written shortly after his death.

GREENE, GRAHAM. *The Lost Childhood*. London: Eyre & Spottiswoode, 1951. Subscribes to the usually held theory about the warping effects of Munro's atypical childhood.

HARTLEY, L. P. "The Collected Works of Saki," *Bookman* (London), LXXI (January, 1927), 214–17. A rather strange appraisal of Munro, which considers his work to be militarily conceived and executed. The review is full of military metaphors.

HINDLE, WILFRID. *The Morning Post 1772–1937*. London: George Routledge & Sons, 1937. Interesting description of this paper's long history. It was almost inevitable that Munro should write for a paper so archetypical of his aristocratic attitudes.

LAMBERT, J. W. "Jungle Boy in the Drawing Room," *Listener* (February 9, 1956), 211–12. Worthy effort to revive interest in Munro. Points out the danger of his work's falling into obscurity.

———. Introduction. *The Bodley Head Saki*. London: The Bodley Head, 1963. The best of the latter-day appreciations, written by one who had special access to Munro's family and publishers. An updated analysis of Munro and his work from the vantage point of the 1960's.

MACQUEEN-POPE, W. *Twenty Shillings in the Pound*. London: Hutchinson & Company, Ltd., 1949. Gives the look and the feel of upper-class London *circa* 1910.

———. *Back Numbers*. London: Hutchinson & Company, Ltd., 1954.

Amplifies the previous book's discussion of early twentieth-century life among the classes and the masses of England.

MAIS, S. P. B. *Books and Their Writers.* London: Grant Richards, 1920. Munro's sister Ethel believed that Mais was the most perceptive of Munro's critics. Certainly the chapter "The Humour of Saki" (pp. 311–30) is an appreciative study.

MARCUS, GEOFFREY. *Before the Lamps Went Out.* Boston-Toronto: Little, Brown and Company, 1965. Most detailed and illuminating picture of life in Great Britain on the brink of World War I.

MAUROIS, ANDRE. *The Edwardian Era.* Trans. Hamish Miles. New York: D. Appleton-Century Company, 1933. French view of the decade 1901–10.

MAY, J. LEWIS. *John Lane and the Nineties.* London: John Lane, The Bodley Head, 1936. A discussion of the literary enterprise and innovations of Munro's last publisher. Munro's 1894 convalescence is presented in some detail.

MONTAGUE, C. E. *Disenchantment.* New York: Brentano, 1925. Like Munro, Montague was a brilliant journalist (*Manchester Guardian*) who enlisted in 1914 when he was well over age. Some of his soul-shaking experiences in the British army may be applied to Munro.

PORTERFIELD, ALEXANDER. "Saki," *London Mercury,* XII (August, 1925), 385–94. Lengthy and very perceptive article; contends that Munro was still contemporaneous in 1925.

PRITCHETT, V. S. "The Performing Lynx," *New Statesman,* LIII (January 5, 1957), 18. The not unusual view that Munro was trying "to get back at the world." Subscribes, too, to the theory of the warped childhood.

———. "Saki," *New Statesman,* LXVI (November 1, 1963), 614. A somewhat disparaging modern view of Munro's work.

REYNOLDS, ROTHAY. *My Russian Year.* New York: James Pott Company, 1912. Useful because it shows much of the Russian background against which Munro worked in 1904–6. Munro knew Reynolds in St. Petersburg.

ROBERTSON SCOTT, J. W. "*'We' and Me.*" London: W. H. Allen, 1956. Discusses the personalities of F. Carruthers Gould and J. A. Spender, Munro's mentors of the *Westminster Alice* period.

SPEARS, G. J. *The Satire of Saki.* New York: Exposition Press, 1963. Proves that there is still some modern critical interest in Munro.

TOYE, FRANCIS. *For What We Have Received.* New York: Alfred A. Knopf, 1948. Gives a detailed picture of the personalities and the editorial policies of the *Bystander* during the period when Munro was contributing to it.

TRAVERS, BEN. *Vale of Laughter.* London: Geoffrey Bles, 1957. Travers worked in John Lane's office when Munro was being published by Lane, and Travers sometimes conversed socially and in a business way with Munro. A most informative account of the workings of the Bodley Head offices in Munro's time.

WINGFIELD-STRATFORD, E. C. *Victorian Aftermath.* New York: Morrow, 1934. Another work, and a good one, on England between 1900 and 1914.

WORSLEY-GOUGH, BARBARA. *Fashions in London.* London: Allan Wingate, 1952. Useful guide to the manners and the amusements of the Best People in Munro's time.

Index

(References to the works of H. H. Munro will be found under his name.)